HOW EQUALITY WINS

HOW EQUALITY WINS

A NEW VISION FOR AN INCLUSIVE AMERICA

Kenji Yoshino and David Glasgow

SIMON ACUMEN
New York   Amsterdam/Antwerp   London
Toronto   Sydney/Melbourne   New Delhi

SIMON
ACUMEN

An Imprint of Simon & Schuster, LLC
1230 Avenue of the Americas
New York, NY 10020

For more than 100 years, Simon & Schuster has championed authors and the stories they create. By respecting the copyright of an author's intellectual property, you enable Simon & Schuster and the author to continue publishing exceptional books for years to come. We thank you for supporting the author's copyright by purchasing an authorized edition of this book.

No amount of this book may be reproduced or stored in any format, nor may it be uploaded to any website, database, language-learning model, or other repository, retrieval, or artificial intelligence system without express permission. All rights reserved. Inquiries may be directed to Simon & Schuster, 1230 Avenue of the Americas, New York, NY 10020 or permissions@simonandschuster.com.

Copyright © 2026 by Kenji Yoshino and David Glasgow

All rights reserved, including the right to reproduce this book or portions thereof in any form whatsoever. For information, address Simon Element Subsidiary Rights Department, 1230 Avenue of the Americas, New York, NY 10020.

This is a work of nonfiction. Some names and other identifying characteristics have been changed.

First Simon Acumen hardcover edition February 2026

SIMON ACUMEN and colophon are registered trademarks of Simon & Schuster, LLC

Simon & Schuster strongly believes in freedom of expression and stands against censorship in all its forms. For more information, visit BooksBelong.com.

For information about special discounts for bulk purchases, please contact Simon & Schuster Special Sales at 1-866-506-1949 or business@simonandschuster.com.

The Simon & Schuster Speakers Bureau can bring authors to your live event. For more information or to book an event, contact the Simon & Schuster Speakers Bureau at 1-866-248-3049 or visit our website at www.simonspeakers.com.

Interior design by Kathryn A. Kenney-Peterson

Manufactured in the United States of America

1 3 5 7 9 10 8 6 4 2

Library of Congress Control Number: 2025949013

ISBN 978-1-6682-1675-0
ISBN 978-1-6682-1676-7 (ebook)

Let's stay in touch! Scan here to get book recommendations, exclusive offers, and more delivered to your inbox.

For Ron, Sophia, and Luke, again and always
And for my sisters Donna, Julie, and Kaye
(KY)

For Andrew, Hugo, and Theodore, who give me hope
(DG)

CONTENTS

Authors' Note	ix
Introduction	1
Strategy 1: **Reveal the Stakes**	15
Strategy 2: **Support Dissent**	30
Strategy 3: **Welcome New Groups**	45
Strategy 4: **Level the Playing Field**	63
Strategy 5: **Embrace the Universal**	79
Strategy 6: **Reclaim Merit**	98
Strategy 7: **Highlight the Risks of Retreat**	113
Conclusion	127
Acknowledgments	135
Additional Legal Resources	139
Notes	141
Reading Group Guide	187

AUTHORS' NOTE

This book is a work of nonfiction. Nonetheless, we changed minor details in some anecdotes (such as proper names or other identifying characteristics) to protect the anonymity of the people involved. For ease of reading, we also used the pronouns "we," "us," and "our" to describe experiences we've had either individually or together in our professional capacities at the Meltzer Center for Diversity, Inclusion, and Belonging.

HOW EQUALITY WINS

INTRODUCTION

On January 29, 2025, a regional jet carrying sixty-four people collided in midair with a helicopter over Washington, D.C., leaving no survivors. When President Donald Trump took the podium the next day to address the grieving nation, the black boxes hadn't been retrieved from the wreckage in the icy Potomac River, much less analyzed. Yet the newly re-elected leader had no qualms about identifying the tragedy's cause: diversity, equity, and inclusion (DEI). The aviation system, he said, required the "highest standards," and the Biden and Obama administrations had settled for "mediocre" ones due to "a big push to put diversity" into the Federal Aviation Administration.

For many defenders of DEI, including us, President Trump's claim was ludicrous. From our perspective, "diversity" refers to making institutions more representative of the talent pool, "equity" means treating people fairly, and "inclusion" is about creating a culture welcoming to all. These values don't cause fatalities.

Yet by the time the president took the podium, DEI had come to stand for something more sinister: identity-based preferences that let individuals without merit coast into positions of power. And because the beneficiaries of DEI were, according to this false framing, less competent, they'd inevitably fail, causing chaos and even death.

By the time of the air crash, blaming any disaster on diversity efforts was a shopworn strategy. When the Francis Scott Key Bridge collapsed in Baltimore after a ship rammed one of its piers in 2024, a Florida politician stated: "DEI did this." As wildfires tore through Los Angeles the following year, billionaire Elon Musk shared footage of the fires on social media with the caption "DEI means people DIE."

The pronouncement on the Potomac, however, differed in kind from its predecessors. It came not from a state politician or businessman, but from the elected leader of the world's most powerful country. As president, Trump could use his bully pulpit and all the levers of the executive branch to mount a crusade against DEI. By the time he made the statement, he'd already started that assault.

On the first day of his second term, President Trump issued an executive order shuttering DEI positions and programs in the federal government—the largest employer in the United States. He followed with a barrage of orders targeting "gender ideology," DEI in the military, and "illegal DEI" in the private sector. Trump tapped vehemently anti-DEI lawyer Harmeet Dhillon to helm the Department of Justice's Civil Rights Division. She stated her mission bluntly: "Either DEI will die on its own, or we will kill it." He elevated another anti-DEI lawyer, Andrea Lucas, to lead the Equal Employment Opportunity Commission (EEOC), the federal agency charged with enforcing laws against employment discrimination. Lucas pledged to immediately start "rooting out unlawful DEI-motivated race and sex discrimination."

These actions were just the opening salvo. One of Trump's executive orders instructed several federal agencies to each identify "up to nine" organizations with DEI programs to target for "civil compliance investigations." The creation of this list harkened back to President Trump's days as a reality TV show host. Leaders of major organizations waited anxiously to find out if they would become one of the unlucky contestants to be fired. Not to be outdone, Attorney General Pam Bondi effectively threatened companies engaged in unlawful DEI with *criminal* investigation. She didn't specify the potential crimes, perhaps because no criminal law could credibly apply to DEI programs. As the months rolled on, the administration advanced more anti-DEI orders, threats, and investigations on topics ranging from "woke" artificial intelligence to "divisive" museum exhibits, underscoring that the obliteration of DEI would be a prime objective of Trump's second term.

In seeking to dismantle DEI, President Trump was in sync with a broader social and legal movement. Anti-DEI advocates like social media influencer Robby Starbuck, legal strategist Edward Blum, political advisor Stephen Miller, and right-wing activist Christopher Rufo were already assailing major corporations, law firms, universities, and even the military, all of which had rightly come to be seen as bastions of DEI. These efforts had pressed many major organizations to publicly retreat from diversity initiatives. Lots more engaged in "diversity hushing" by quietly moving their programs underground.

Though it sometimes flew under the radar, the United States Supreme Court served as the president's most important ally. In 2023, the court issued the seismic *Students for Fair Admissions v. Harvard* decision, which effectively abolished racially conscious admissions in higher education. In doing so, the court's six-member conservative majority provided a clear window into how they were thinking about race discrimination in ways that will have aftershocks for decades to come.

Specifically, the court signaled a shift away from one vision of civil rights law toward another. Under the first vision, which scholars call the "anti-subordination" view, it's sometimes acceptable to treat people differently based on race when it breaks down historical patterns of oppression. Jim Crow segregation laws were illegal because they trampled on marginalized groups, while affirmative action was legal because it aimed to remedy those harms. In the words of the late Justice John Paul Stevens, the difference between Jim Crow and affirmative action is the difference between a "No Trespassing" sign and a "welcome mat."

In its 2023 decision, the court rejected that approach to embrace what scholars call the "anti-classification" view. Under this view, popularly known as "colorblindness," race-based distinctions are inherently problematic and presumptively illegal, even if they benefit marginalized people or promote other laudable goals like diversity.

It's hard to overstate how drastically this shift altered the legal landscape. The anti-subordination view honors the original intention of civil rights laws, which was to lift up historically marginalized communities. The anti-classification view, by contrast, permits the cruel irony of civil rights laws being used to attack minority groups and further empower dominant ones. The court's decision means that No Trespassing signs and welcome mats are now basically the same. Policies that discriminate against the majority are just as legally suspect as policies that discriminate against a minority.

Given that six life-tenured justices voted for it, the anti-classification vision of discrimination law is likely to endure for a generation or more. Moreover, while the Harvard decision was limited to higher education, the court's reasoning has clear implications for employment, contracting, grantmaking, and other domains. In fact, the court has already partially extended its logic to the employment context in a subsequent decision. Smelling blood in the water, conservative legal organizations have started a feeding frenzy, suing a slew of firms, corporations, nonprofits, and governmental entities to challenge their diversity policies.

By early 2025, anti-DEI activists were ecstatic. They'd filed scores of lawsuits, persuaded the president to release a wave of executive orders, stacked federal agencies with DEI opponents, and caused some of America's leading institutions to cave or cower. Even progressives began to turn on DEI, voicing long-suppressed criticisms about how DEI was too co-opted by corporations, too feckless, or too performative. Some commentators drew what seemed to be the unmistakable conclusion: DEI is dead.

THE ENDURING VALUE OF EQUALITY

In the face of this concerted attack on DEI, advocates of equality might easily despair. That would be a mistake. Whether the acronym DEI survives, the value of equality that undergirds it is still stubbornly and inspiringly alive.

What our society has come to call DEI is just the latest embodiment of a project of advancing equality that goes back centuries. That deeper, more durable project has traveled under different banners in different eras, including "equality," "dignity," "fairness," and "opportunity," or "civil rights" and "human rights." And as we look at the past, present, and future of this country, we have every reason to believe this project will endure.

Let's begin with the past. The sweep of American history suggests the ideal of equality has staying power, even in periods of wrenching strife. While the U.S. Constitution speaks of "We, the people," that collective was limited from the outset by group-based exclusions. Our nation was founded on the assumption that a small cadre of white, propertied men would run it. The work of every generation since then has been, often at the cost of immeasurable suffering, to expand who counts as part of the "We." After the Civil War, the Thirteenth Amendment abolished slavery, the Fourteenth guaranteed "the equal protection of the laws," and the Fifteenth granted the franchise to people of color, laying the foundation for subsequent activism during the 1960s civil rights era. The Nineteenth Amendment guaranteed women suffrage, and successive waves of feminism led to an expansion of their rights and opportunities. The post-Stonewall LGBTQ+ movement won sexual minorities greater inclusion, such as employment protections and marriage equality. The disability rights movement fought for, and achieved, legal protections in the Rehabilitation Act of 1973, which were significantly increased with the passage of the Americans with Disabilities Act of 1990.

More recently, the murder of George Floyd in May 2020 ignited what's likely the largest protest movement in our nation's history. The Black Lives Matter movement, combined with the #MeToo movement two years earlier, galvanized leaders of major institutions. They trumpeted their commitment to social justice, hired diversity professionals, established racial and gender equity task forces, announced ambitious diversity targets and philanthropic commitments, and demanded that suppliers meet diversity benchmarks to earn their business. Teachers and administrators from preschool to graduate school scrambled to diversify their ranks and create more inclusive classrooms. Some proclaimed this head-spinning change a social revolution—the "Great Awokening."

Over the centuries, advocates of equality have fought the scourges of slavery, segregation, voter suppression, internment, legalized domestic violence, sexual harassment, rampant workplace discrimination, and cycles of political and vigilante violence. Through it all, the value of equality endured. Focusing too narrowly on the recent defeats relating to DEI obscures that panorama. Given that the equality ideal has survived the most horrific assaults, it seems wildly unlikely that this is the moment the project shudders to a halt. A spirit of inclusion is part of our proud national heritage, which should be a solace and resource to us in times when that value is under siege.

Turning to the present, the value of equality is embedded in the national psyche and in the organizations that structure our daily lives. Multiple public opinion polls conducted in 2024 and 2025 showed roughly half to two-thirds of the country in support of DEI programs, despite the smear campaign against them. Even when Americans express unease about the acronym DEI, they firmly embrace the values it describes. A Siena College Research Institute survey in late 2024 found that while only 50 percent of respondents favored efforts to promote "DEI," that number rocketed to 80 percent when respondents were asked whether they support "having diverse workplaces," "equitable sharing of power in community meetings," and "including people of all backgrounds when discussing the state of our nation." An *Axios* poll in January 2025 similarly found that 61 percent agreed "diverse employees have a positive impact on organizations" and 75 percent agreed "more needs to be done to guarantee everyone is advancing."

Ideas of inclusion and diversity also permeate everyday institutions, including schools, universities, foundations, nonprofits, and corporations. The Heritage Foundation, a conservative think tank, discovered to its chagrin in December 2024 that 486 companies in the Fortune 500 had diversity statements or commitments on their websites. To be sure, that number is unquestionably lower now. As the media is fond of reporting, many companies have retreated from DEI under legal and political pressure. What makes fewer headlines is that most companies that have sidled away from the acronym continue to affirm the values of DEI under a different name. In announcing a shift in strategy, Harley-Davidson said it would continue "to ensure we have an employee base that reflects our customers and the geographies in which we operate." Boeing stated that it maintains "procedures aimed at encouraging an equality of opportunity." Lowe's proclaimed that it remained "committed to fostering an environment where all individuals are welcomed, valued, and respected." These statements sure sound like diversity, equity, and inclusion to us. The education sector is equally if not more committed:

an April 2025 review of 262 colleges and universities found that 245 of them still maintained DEI offices and programs.

Looking to the future, demographic change will make the work of equality indispensable for anyone seeking to navigate an increasingly complex society. More than half of Americans under the age of eighteen are people of color, with some demographers predicting a "majority-minority" nation in the 2040s. More than a quarter of adults in Generation Z (those born between 1997 and 2012) identify as part of the LGBTQ+ community. Women outnumber men in the college-educated workforce. Globalization will continue to ensure students and workers routinely interact with people from a dizzying array of linguistic and cultural backgrounds.

The increasing diversity of our nation will heighten the need for all of us to speak, to learn, and to work across our differences. Institutions that want to recruit the best talent will need to find qualified people in unfamiliar places. Organizations that want to market goods to diverse consumers will need to communicate with cultural savvy. Schools and universities will need to create inclusive classrooms and help students navigate identity-related conflicts. Workplaces will need leaders who understand how to manage diverse teams and address barriers to equal opportunity in hiring and promotion. Whatever label you attach to this work, the project of building more inclusive and egalitarian institutions will become an even more essential endeavor for the foreseeable future.

THE IRRESISTIBLE FORCE MEETS THE IMMOVABLE OBJECT

Our current moment evokes a famous paradox: "What happens when the irresistible force meets the immovable object?"

The legal and social war on DEI feels like an irresistible force. On the legal side, the Trump White House, and key agencies like the Department of Justice and the EEOC, are laser-focused on dismantling DEI programs across the public and private sectors. More profoundly, the conservative Supreme Court's interpretations of the law have shackled how the work of equality can proceed. On the social side, the cultural landscape has become considerably more hostile to DEI compared to the early 2020s. It would be foolish for those of us who care about equality to think we can carry on with the work of DEI exactly as we did before.

At the same time, the widespread social commitment to the value of equality is an immovable object. No matter what federal policies are enacted or court decisions are handed down, whole generations of Americans have grown up with the bedrock understanding that all human beings are created equal. They've entered marriages and formed deep friendships across their racial, ethnic, and religious differences. They've bonded with family members, neighbors, and colleagues who are openly LGBTQ+ or disabled. They've absorbed a diversity of human narratives through television, film, and other media that would have been unimaginable in earlier times. While the field of DEI is in crisis, too many Americans prize the venerable ideal of equality for it to disappear.

The question is what will happen when the irresistible force of the assault on DEI meets the immovable object of the collective commitment to equality. Our answer to the riddle is that the work of equality will have to change. This will mean the force isn't resisted, but absorbed. And it will mean the object isn't moved, but transformed. To survive, this project will need to absorb the shock of the anti-DEI movement, and morph into something new.

A RECOMMITMENT TO EQUALITY

This book is a blueprint and manifesto for what that "something new" should look like. We offer a distinctive take on this topic, because we run one of the only research centers focused on the field of inclusion that operates out of a major law school. Kenji is the faculty director and David is the executive director of the Meltzer Center for Diversity, Inclusion, and Belonging at NYU School of Law. Kenji has spent a quarter of a century teaching and writing at the intersection of constitutional law and antidiscrimination law. David is a former employment discrimination lawyer who spent years advising companies on how to create respectful workplaces. Both of us are experts in the law of equal opportunity. We maintain a public educational tracker of all federal DEI lawsuits, publish and comment extensively on the current landscape for diversity work in academic and popular forums, and teach and counsel thousands of leaders across industries on how to craft lawful equality programs.

That legal knowledge is critical for building a lasting vision of equality. The law used to operate as the "floor" above which the work of DEI was conducted. It provided a foundation of basic protections against discrimination, while DEI tried to build a flourishing culture of inclusion on top of it. When the Supreme Court and the Trump administration waged a legal battle against this work, the law came to operate more like a "ceiling" crashing down on the entire enterprise.

Many people were caught off guard by this shift. Most lawyers didn't understand the work of DEI. Most DEI practitioners didn't understand the law. We were—and still are—alarmed by this knowledge gap, because it leads to ruinous effects in both directions. Some proponents of diversity confidently assert that the Supreme Court's affirmative action decision has no implications for DEI, leaving organizations completely exposed to lawsuits. Some opponents, with equal assurance, say all DEI is illegal, leading many organizations to jettison perfectly lawful and valuable initiatives. A basic understanding of the law in this area is no longer a nice-to-have. It's essential for anyone who wants this work to survive.

In addition to our legal expertise, we've become acutely sensitive to how this field is received in the court of public opinion. Our work puts us in regular contact with liberal student activists on the one hand, and risk-averse corporate leaders on the other. We've engaged on issues of inclusion and diversity with tens of thousands of people from all walks of life—from Fortune 500 CEOs to university administrators to nonprofit leaders to lawyers to small business owners to activists to athletes to farmers to government employees to construction workers to high school students to Broadway performers. Those conversations have taught us not just which diversity programs and language will find favor with the Supreme Court, but also which ones resonate with the American people.

This book reimagines DEI so the work of equality can weather the legal and social backlash to emerge stronger on the other side. Given that we regard DEI as one incarnation of a broader ideal, we'll generally refer to the subject of this book as the "project of equality" rather than DEI, or sometimes simply as "equality" or "equal opportunity."

This project can be captured in four simple tenets. First, equality is a birthright, because all human beings are equal in moral worth. Second, equality is both material and dignitary—it's about the fair allocation of resources, but it's also about reducing stigma and enhancing respect for each other as human beings across our differences. Third, equality remains an unrealized promise for many historically marginalized groups, including but not limited to people of color, women, LGBTQ+ people, and disabled people. Finally, equality won't be realized just by putting in place formal rules of equal treatment—organizations should take positive steps to undo bias and promote fairness. We consider anyone who endorses these four tenets to be on the side of the project of equality, regardless of partisan political affiliation. By contrast, people of many different ideologies oppose this project, including those who deny the equal moral worth of all human beings, those who think only material equality matters, those who think society is already fair, and those who think nothing should be done to address inequality.

Our book shares the traditional focus of DEI, looking specifically at "organizational equality" rather than broader questions of how to create a fairer society overall. We won't discuss how to design a just immigration regime, electoral system, or tax code. Instead, we focus on ensuring greater fairness and equal opportunity in organizations, including workplaces, universities, K-12 schools, foundations, community centers, houses of worship, sports leagues, neighborhood associations, and nonprofit advocacy groups.

We focus on organizational equality because this is where most individuals can make a difference. Few of us draft civil rights legislation or start social movements. But all of us can make change in the communities in which we live, work, worship, or socialize. We hope this book will speak to any employee who wants their workplace to treat them with respect, any parent on the PTA who cares about building a welcoming environment at their child's elementary school, any volunteer at a nonprofit organization or neighborhood association who wants to create a program to help disadvantaged groups, any student or administrator at a university who wants to admit a more diverse student body, and any small business owner who wants to develop fair policies for their employees. Indeed, because it concerns how we treat each other in our daily interactions, the pursuit of equality requires such broad participation across society.

Our practical bent also leads us to keep our conceptual discussion of equality to a minimum. We're not interested in grand theories that leave readers inspired but confused about what to do next. We instead share tangible guidance on how to reshape equality practices. To that end, this book lays out seven strategies to enable the project of equality to thrive over the next generation.

THE SEVEN STRATEGIES

Our strategies are grouped into three broad categories, each with a different emphasis.

The first two strategies offer reforms to how supporters of equality engage with both sides of this debate. Strategy 1: Reveal the Stakes urges such supporters to expose the other side's extremism, hypocrisy, and tortured logic so that persuadable Americans reject their agenda. Strategy 2: Support Dissent critiques our movement's own extreme tendencies, urging supporters of equality to embrace free speech, welcome debate, and avoid shaming people for mistakes.

The next three strategies offer a substantive reconstruction of the project of equality. Strategy 3: Welcome New Groups urges the project to include more social groups, using religious individuals, boys and men, and people from lower socioeconomic backgrounds as case studies. Strategy 4: Level the Playing Field explores how the work can move from "lifting" approaches that confer group preferences to "leveling" approaches that even out the playing field for everyone. Strategy 5: Embrace the Universal discusses how equality programs can mitigate legal and social risks by allowing everyone to participate.

The final two strategies explore how proponents of equality can communicate more effectively. Strategy 6: Reclaim Merit urges supporters not to allow opponents to use "merit" against us, but rather to make clear how the ideal of merit and the ideal of equality go together. Strategy 7: Highlight the Risks of Retreat encourages supporters to remind doubters why this work remains indispensable, and why hastily retreating from the project of equality contains its own downsides.

Some of the shifts we recommend—like reducing language-policing and putting greater emphasis on free speech—may appeal more to moderate or conservative readers. Other shifts—like making the work of equality deeper and more pervasive than it was before—are likely to appeal to progressives. We'll doubtless frustrate you at times, so this might be a good place to note that the strategies need not be accepted as a package deal. Whether you agree or disagree with individual chapters, we hope the book will prompt you to think and talk with other supporters of equality about the future direction of this movement.

HOW WE WIN

There's an old labor activist saying often misattributed to Mahatma Gandhi: "First they ignore you, then they laugh at you, then they fight you, then you win." The initial beats in this quote aptly describe our journey in the field of DEI. When we launched our center a decade ago, many of our colleagues didn't even know what DEI was. Then they learned what it was, but found it bizarre that two lawyers had chosen to work on such a "soft" subject. Now, no one is laughing. They realize the fight over DEI is a fight for the identity and soul of the nation.

Aside from describing our own experience in this work, this quote also resonates with us for its reminder that having coordinated forces arrayed against you is a sign of strength. Opponents are fighting DEI not because of its failure, but because of its astounding success.

Yet we've always felt ambivalent about the final statement, "then you win," for its seeming belief in the inevitability of victory. Even in our increasingly diverse society, victory isn't a foregone conclusion. Nor is it ever permanent. After President Barack Obama's election in 2008, many assumed a rainbow coalition of women, voters of color, and young voters would all but guarantee the triumph of an inclusive and cosmopolitan vision of the world. In 2024, President Trump burst that iridescent bubble. Even though his agenda was antithetical to DEI, he won the popular vote with an increase in support among women, voters of color, and young voters compared to his 2016 victory.

The notion that "demography is destiny" rested on the faulty premise that as the population became less white, less Christian, and more visibly LGBTQ+, the rising numbers of Americans from historically marginalized groups would inevitably see their interests best served by an agenda built around recognizing and uplifting people of different identities. Many acolytes of this article of faith didn't anticipate other possibilities: What if those Americans found aspects of the DEI agenda off-putting? What if they saw their own group's interests as distinct from others' in the rainbow coalition? What if they started to view themselves primarily through a class-based lens, drawn to populist leaders who promised to take on an out-of-touch liberal establishment? What if group members climbed the ladder of progress, then pulled it up after themselves?

Victory for the project of equality won't depend on the mere passage of time. Instead, it will depend on how we collectively think about this movement, how we talk about it, and how we implement our ideals. Our movement must tap into the values that most Americans hold dear. It must avoid the messages and tactics that fuel the opposition. And it must clarify the pivotal choice at hand: whether to embrace a vision of America rooted in dominance with some groups at the top of the social hierarchy and others at the bottom, or a vision that upholds the equal dignity of all.

We're clear-eyed about the daunting barriers faced by champions of equality at this moment in history. But our predecessors faced their own daunting barriers and stayed in the fight. We owe it to previous generations to continue the work. And we owe it to future ones to ensure our nation doesn't just live under its highest ideals, but truly lives up to them.

Strategy 1:
REVEAL THE STAKES

We launched our research center two days after the 2016 presidential election. In the months of planning, we thought it was an auspicious time to launch a center dedicated to issues of diversity, inclusion, and belonging. The ice seemed to be finally breaking on long-standing forms of inequality, opening new pathways for our work. Hillary Clinton was favored to become the first woman president of the United States, succeeding the first Black president. To mark this historic moment, we invited Justice Sonia Sotomayor—the first woman of color and first Hispanic person to serve on the Supreme Court—to speak at our launch, and she agreed.

Then, to the shock of many, Donald Trump defeated Hillary Clinton. Trump had spent the campaign railing against many of the values our center had been established to advance. He called Mexican immigrants drug dealers and rapists, called for a "total and complete shutdown of Muslims entering the United States," and made crude misogynistic comments about women. Although our law school community holds a variety of political opinions, we knew the people showing up to a launch event for a diversity center in New York City would be, on the whole, devastated by the election result.

We were right. As four hundred and fifty attendees filed into the law school auditorium, the mood felt funereal. From the front of the room, we saw row upon row of haggard and ashen faces. People came up to us all night, shook our hands, and conveyed messages of pessimism mixed with steely determination. "The next four years will be tough," they said. "You have your work cut out for you."

For all the challenges of President Trump's first term, however, it was also a boon for DEI. Advocates mobilized on a mass scale around issues like gender equality, racial justice, and trans rights. As former EEOC commissioner and lawyer Jenny R. Yang put it to us, people took to the streets because they lacked faith that the government would protect their interests.

By the end of Trump's first term, and in the immediate years after President Joe Biden took office, the DEI movement was triumphant. Its opponents felt crushed under the weight of their seemingly invincible enemy. In her 2022 book *How Woke Won*, columnist Joanna Williams lamented: "From schools and universities to multinational corporations, social media, journalism, and even the police and military, woke values dominate every aspect of our lives." Right-wing author Richard Hanania similarly argued in 2023 that in institutions, "the identity-obsessed left has all the power." The dominance of the DEI agenda at that time is perhaps best captured by the subtitle of activist Christopher Rufo's 2023 book *America's Cultural Revolution*, which reads: *How the Radical Left Conquered Everything*.

Yet the anti-DEI forces didn't just sit on their hands. They forged ahead, mounting a full-scale incursion into the cultural terrain that DEI occupied. As part of that incursion, they made two strategic choices that still shape the public narrative.

First, opponents refused to accept our rendering of what DEI means. To supporters, DEI is almost self-evidently valuable. As politician Pete Buttigieg observed in a conversation with a voter: "DEI stands for diversity, equity, inclusion. So to me, we start by thinking, what's the opposite of those things? The opposite of diversity is uniformity. The opposite of equity is inequity. And the opposite of inclusion is exclusion. And I don't know a lot of people who think we'd be better off if our lives had more uniformity, inequity, and exclusion." Opponents flipped this script, claiming that DEI stands for "discrimination, exclusion, and intolerance." They framed DEI supporters as extreme, suggesting we consist of Marxists, critical race theorists, and other assorted radicals. They highlighted the most militant figures in our movement and styled them as our spokespeople. They attacked every component of our core arguments.

Second, opponents of DEI portrayed their own side's agenda in terms that appealed to moderates. While slamming the idea of "equity," conservative lawyer and writer Sarah Parshall Perry lauded the maxim that all individuals are "created equal," calling it "fundamental to our nation's founding." Legal strategist Edward Blum, who has brought multiple lawsuits challenging diversity programs, said he hoped for the "restoration of the great colorblind covenant that has held together this country through very difficult periods of history." Utah governor Spencer Cox defended his state's anti-DEI law by invoking the "immortal words of Dr. King" that our children should "not be judged by the color of their skin, but by the content of their character." And Christopher Rufo called for "a regime of full colorblind equality" dedicated to the "equal treatment of individuals under law, according to their talents and virtues, rather than their ancestry and anatomy."

This two-pronged approach has been astonishingly successful at setting the terms of the debate. Opponents have recognized that the war over DEI is about a choice: What kind of society do we all want to live in? They've successfully framed the choice as between colorblind equality and radical far-left identity politics. This frame gaslights the American public. The actual choice is different. On one side is the project of equality. On the other side is 1950s gender roles, ostracism of LGBTQ+ people, and a racial order that relegates people of color to the margins of society. The public conversation about DEI would be dramatically different if the stakes were clearly identified in this way.

To expose the real stakes, supporters of DEI need to scrutinize opponents' asserted commitment to a regime of full colorblind equality. Three litmus tests will help. First, people who sincerely believe in colorblind equality should full-throatedly endorse the equal dignity of all human beings in public and private. Second, they should acknowledge that the status quo in our nation isn't yet fair for historically marginalized groups. Third, they should take action to address inequalities in *all* directions to achieve the goal of colorblind equality, not selectively take action only when it benefits dominant groups.

Many skeptics of DEI pass these litmus tests. They're reasonable, moderate people who believe in equality but have qualms about how the field of DEI has pursued that goal. Not only do we welcome the opinions of this group, but we also actively engage with their critiques to improve our work. But many opponents miserably fail at least one of these tests. Supporters of equality should shine a spotlight on this second group, relentlessly exposing their extremism, flimsy arguments, and hypocrisy in conversations with persuadable friends, neighbors, and colleagues. If the American people get a clear picture of what the country would look like without the project of equality, we believe they will recoil.

ARE THEY FOR EQUALITY?

Many opponents flunk the first question. The *New York Times* gave us an unsettling view into the strange twilight world of anti-DEI crusaders when it reported on their private correspondence. The article revealed that Scott Yenor, a college professor and fellow at the right-wing Claremont Institute, endorsed the views that "a healthy society requires patriarchy" and that "our sexual culture will not heal until 'faggot' replaces 'bigot' as the slur of choice." Yenor also described imprisonment of gay people as a "wholesome" policy. The article then featured Heather Mac Donald of the Manhattan Institute, who found it objectionable that women lawyers were handing over care of their children to nannies of color from "the low IQ 3rd world."

Some of the crusaders engaged in dual messaging. They agreed among themselves that they wanted to protect the job of an embattled law professor, Amy Wax. Wax was under investigation for what her law school dean called "intentional and incessant racist, sexist, xenophobic, and homophobic actions and statements" that, in his view, had led faculty and students to fairly believe they would experience "discriminatory animus" if they encountered her. Yenor gave advice to his friend David Azerrad, also a professor, on how to defend Wax to a liberal audience using the principle of academic freedom: "You are appealing to lefties, so you should target them, both on free speech grounds and on grounds that implicate their fears." He encouraged Azerrad to argue that if Wax were fired, it would embolden Republican states to fire controversial left-wing professors. "Don't we want this to happen?" Azerrad

STRATEGY 1: REVEAL THE STAKES

replied. "Yes," said Yenor, "but your audience doesn't want it to happen." While "academic freedom" provided a convenient talking point, a separate email from two years earlier offers a clue as to the possible deeper motivations at play. Yenor declared: "The core of what we oppose is 'anti-discrimination.'" Yet he noted that anti-discrimination was "too much of a sacred cow." At least for now.

Some anti-DEI figures don't bother with subterfuge. Even though Yenor so fastidiously defended her, Wax herself has had no qualms about saying the quiet part out loud. She has argued publicly that women are "less intellectual than men," that "on average, Blacks have lower cognitive ability than whites," and that "there is something to be said for" the view that "our country will be better off with more whites and fewer nonwhites." Trump State Department appointee Darren Beattie once posted on social media that "competent white men must be in charge if you want things to work." Laura Loomer, a right-wing activist influential in the Trump administration, referred to Black women leaders like Vice President Kamala Harris, New York Attorney General Letitia James, and Fulton County District Attorney Fani Willis as having "little DEI Shaniqua voices" and being "meritless DEI Shaniquas."

These perspectives are hardly unique. Political commentator and DEI opponent Candace Owens has observed that "every ill that we are fighting right now in society has been brought forth by women." Conservative podcast host Matt Walsh, who created a documentary satirizing DEI, has described a family "headed up by two gay men" as an "abomination," and has said that a child going to two gay parents is "easily worse" than being in foster care. And Secretary of Defense Pete Hegseth, one of the Trump administration's most tenacious warriors in the battle against DEI, has shared a video online in which pastors said women shouldn't be able to vote and same-sex sexual intimacy should be illegal. Hegseth has also called for an "insurgency" to "discredit the public school system" and ultimately ensure "classical Christian education" provides "the core of America's education." This isn't the behavior we'd expect from people committed to the equality of all human beings.

DO THEY ACKNOWLEDGE THAT THE STATUS QUO ISN'T FAIR?

Even those who say they believe in equality routinely fail our second litmus test by refusing to acknowledge ongoing unfairness in our society.

On the first day of a course we were teaching on leadership, diversity, and inclusion, we opened with some statistics. Seventy-four percent of Fortune 50 CEOs were white men, even though white men comprised only 30 percent of the U.S. population. Four percent of such CEOs were Black, in contrast to 14 percent of the population. Panning out a bit, Fortune 50 executives were 65 percent male and 74 percent white, law firm equity partners were 75 percent male and 90 percent white, and members of Congress were 72 percent male and 74 percent white. We used these statistics to set up the problem of inequality that our course sought to address.

At that point, a student piped up. "Why do we need to be the ones coming up with solutions?" he asked. "Why aren't we making opponents of DEI justify these discrepancies? What story could they possibly tell about these numbers other than one about an appalling level of bias?"

To which we could only say: amen. When blatant demographic disparities favor historically dominant groups in arenas of power like business, law, and politics, supporters of the equality project have a clear story. We believe such disparities exist because historically marginalized groups continue to face barriers on the path to the most powerful positions in society. Those barriers could be explicit, like discrimination. They could involve subtle impediments, like stereotypes, or a lack of confidence that comes from being underrepresented in a particular field. They could be due to structural factors, like a dearth of economic or educational opportunity that makes it harder to attain the knowledge and skills necessary to enter those domains. No matter the specific cause, we believe vast statistical gaps should raise eyebrows and prompt organizations to act. Institutions should gather data to discern whether barriers are indeed holding back certain groups, and if so, remove those barriers.

STRATEGY 1: REVEAL THE STAKES

Opponents of the equality project, on the other hand, engage in intellectual gymnastics. Most of them don't want to say white men simply have more merit than other groups—a blatantly racist and misogynistic argument. They also don't want to say it's easier for white men to advance to leadership roles than other groups, which would undermine their whole case against DEI. If anything, they need to maintain that the odds are currently stacked *against* white men, as white men are supposedly the victims of DEI-related discrimination. So they're in a bit of a pickle. How exactly, according to their view, could white men be so disproportionately in control of the levers of power in our society?

Some respond with stout denial. In his 2024 book *Go Woke, Go Broke*, journalist Charles Gasparino claims that "until recently, there's been a near ban on hiring and promoting white men at many large corporations." All we can say about this view is: when we look at the numbers, the "near ban" has been an abysmal failure.

Others dodge the question. In an interview, Edward Blum was asked if he believed in systemic racism. The interviewer made an empirical case: "If you look at statistics in this country, a typical white family holds ten times the wealth that a typical Black family does. There are currently only eight Black CEOs of Fortune 500 companies, twenty Latino CEOs. Black people live sicker lives and they die younger than white people. I could go on." Blum responded: "No, I do not believe in it. What your question implies is that in the American DNA there is racism. It was founded upon racism. It is part of what this country is. I reject that." This response is a raging non-sequitur. The interviewer was citing statistics about present disparities, not making any claim that the United States was immutably racist. Notably, Blum never contested the accuracy of the statistics or explained why those statistics didn't indicate the existence of structural racism.

The remaining opponents who at least feel some pressure to grapple with empirical reality have a go-to response that we call the "basketball objection." Here's author Coleman Hughes: "Is anyone suspicious about seventy-five percent of NBA players being black? Does anyone accuse the NBA recruitment system of anti-white racism? No. . . . If it turns out that most of the best players are black, then so be it." Rufo also cites the "heavily Black representation in the NBA," and adds other examples into the mix: "I think most people accept that when they go to the nail salon and it's being run by almost all Vietnamese people, they're fine with that. When you go to a programming floor it's mostly East Asian and South Asian males and white males." He elaborates: "The world is complicated and most people have a sense that different groups, different cultures, have different priorities, different interests, different talents, and they don't mathematically graft themselves in an artificial way onto every institution." The implication of this argument—rarely stated directly—is that white men are just more interested in, or talented at, wielding economic and political power, while other groups tend to be better at playing basketball or painting nails.

The problem with the basketball objection is that it treats group differences as springing naturally from some cultural essence, as though professional decisions aren't shaped by the environments in which people make them. Indeed, the basketball objection arguably cuts in the opposite direction from how Hughes and Rufo seek to deploy it. Sportswriter Reagan Griffin Jr. offers other plausible explanations for why Black individuals are overrepresented in some athletic pursuits like basketball. One is that compared with sports like baseball, tennis, and golf that have high economic barriers to entry, basketball is more accessible to people who are disproportionately economically disadvantaged. Another is that pervasive bias and stereotyping have led many Black kids to grow up with a "burning desire to become professional athletes" out of a belief that sports are "the only way out, the only road to making something of themselves." These explanations don't regard the overrepresentation of Black individuals in the NBA as a story of racial neutrality. They regard it as evidence of economic disadvantage and systemic racism.

Rufo's example about Vietnamese people running nail salons is similarly flawed. After the Vietnam War, Vietnamese refugees sought to survive economically in the United States. They chose a trade that was relatively easy to learn, had low startup costs, and didn't require strong English language skills. This initial influx also created path dependency, where subsequent waves of immigrants entered the industry because they knew their likelihood of success there would be greater. Again, a marginalized community gravitating toward accessible pursuits because it's too hard to break into other occupations reinforces the need for the project of equality, rather than undermining it.

Even if we accepted that some groups favor different pursuits for innocuous reasons, opponents of the equality project would still have some explaining to do. Let's grant for the sake of argument that Asian and white men are more likely to be interested in tech because they happen to like working with computers, that women tend to be better at nursing or teaching because they happen to be more nurturing on average than men, and that Black individuals are culturally drawn to basketball while white people are drawn to golf and tennis. As long as no one is discriminated against in these domains, these group disparities are no big deal, right?

Well, for starters, we know that certain groups do experience bias and discrimination when entering domains in which they're underrepresented. In a 2024 study, 57 percent of women in tech fields reported having experienced gender bias in the workplace including sexist comments, harassment, gender pay gaps, and being passed up for promotion in favor of less qualified men. The work of organizational equality is precisely to uncover these kinds of barriers—both overt and subtle—that preclude underrepresented groups from receiving a fair shake when they enter counter-stereotypical environments. A cavalier, nothing-to-see-here attitude that treats glaring disparities as harmless group preferences gives up the pursuit of equal opportunity without even trying.

More deeply, even if we were comfortable with, say, Vietnamese women dominating nail salons, we'd still be uncomfortable with white men dominating the political and corporate elite. When some groups prefer salsa dancing and others prefer ballet, or some groups gravitate toward equestrian sports while others embrace soccer, no group necessarily gains any economic, political, or social advantage over others. But when one group dominates legislatures or corporate boards, that group then exercises power over others and sets the legal and economic conditions for the rest of the country. That's why diversity advocates care more about diversifying the federal judiciary than they do about diversifying lacrosse leagues.

Conservative opponents of DEI should understand this point. When they complain about the "liberal media" or the lack of viewpoint diversity in academia, they wouldn't accept an answer that says "different groups have different priorities, and liberal people just happen to pursue journalism and academia more than conservatives." Rather, they'd say news outlets and universities exercise tremendous power over society and shape the narratives that influence millions of Americans, so those institutions should better reflect the diversity of the nation.

The argument that groups have different preferences that are neither here nor there also raises a more subtle problem. An assertion that "Asians have a culture of valuing STEM" while "Black people have a culture of valuing athletics" suggests that race is a "thick" characteristic, meaning it's not just a superficial matter of ancestry or skin color, but rather a deeper trait with associated histories, cultures, attitudes, and behaviors.

Yet anti-DEI advocates rejected exactly that premise in their crusade against affirmative action. In their view, it's insulting to assume anything about a person's attitudes or behaviors due to their race. The reason we're all supposed to be "colorblind" is that race is a "thin" characteristic that tells us nothing about an individual. As the Supreme Court observed in its *Students for Fair Admissions* decision, it's a "pernicious stereotype" to assume in college admissions that "a black student can usually bring something that a white person cannot offer."

Anti-DEI folks need to pick a lane. If race is a thin characteristic that says nothing about an individual, then race would be like the letter of the alphabet with which your surname begins. If that's the case, why wouldn't we all expect, in the absence of bias, that racial groups would enter into professions roughly in line with their numbers in the general population? Conversely, if race is a thick characteristic that leads some racial groups to be better at basketball or programming, then why reject race-based diversity arguments for affirmative action?

What emerges from this brief survey is that opponents of the project of equality get tied up in knots when confronted with empirical proof of inequality. They deny, deflect, or deploy weak arguments like the basketball objection that crumble under scrutiny. We suspect that underneath it all, many opponents believe it's fine that historically dominant groups still hold disproportionate political, economic, and social power. If that's what they truly think, they shouldn't be able to use shoddy reasoning to evade saying so.

ARE THEY CONSISTENT IN FIGHTING FOR EQUALITY?

Let's say someone is for equality and acknowledges that society remains unfair for marginalized groups. A reasonable follow-up litmus test is: Do they sincerely champion equality for such marginalized groups, or do they only care about equality when it upholds traditional social hierarchies?

In the Supreme Court's 2023 affirmative action decision, for instance, the court stated in ringing tones that "eliminating racial discrimination means eliminating all of it." Whenever we read this line, we wistfully think how extraordinary it would be if society delivered on that project not only for white men, but for everyone. It would mean fighting every instance of systemic, conscious, and unconscious bias that disadvantages people of all backgrounds. And it's not an unreasonable expectation. After all, the anti-DEI crusaders (at least the moderate ones) don't say, "We believe in fairness, but only for whites or men."

Yet in our experience, many such crusaders speak up for people of color or women only when using them to benefit dominant groups or to drive a wedge between marginalized ones. In the debates over affirmative action, activists seemed to care deeply about discrimination against Asian Americans, but only when Asian Americans could serve the interests of the white majority. If we look at the "model plaintiffs" who have challenged affirmative action at the Supreme Court, we see white male plaintiffs in the 1970s and '80s. We then see a shift toward white female plaintiffs like Barbara Grutter or Abigail Fisher in the 2000s and 2010s, who were presumably more sympathetic because they had encountered disadvantages as women. In the *Students for Fair*

Admissions case, activists perfected the strategy by bringing forward Asian plaintiffs, pitting one racial group (Asian individuals) against another (Black individuals). It's of course true that Asian Americans can be harmed by some forms of affirmative action. Yet we see little evidence that the people leading the charge against affirmative action have devoted their energies to fighting anti-Asian discrimination outside this context.

Similarly, when Kenji testified before Congress in defense of the Equality Act (a bill that would have extended employment discrimination protections to LGBTQ+ individuals), he was struck by how often opponents of the Act claimed to be defending women. While the bill didn't explicitly address the topic of trans women's participation in athletics, opponents repeatedly said they resisted the bill because they wanted to protect women's sports. After listening to these rousing defenses, Representative Ted Deutch observed that it was "frankly rich" for representatives who spend their time in Congress "doing everything they can to limit the ability of women to make their own choices about their own bodies" to now champion women's rights. Getting red in the face, Representative Louie Gohmert, an opponent of the bill, responded that he was "a father of three girls" and had coached his daughters in sports. Gohmert notably didn't point to any other legislative work he'd done to advance women's rights.

We suppose it's encouraging that some opponents of the equality project feel pressure to *claim* to stick up for historically marginalized groups like Asian Americans and women, even if they do so opportunistically. At other times, the hypocrisy is even more blatant.

Take Christopher Rufo, who has called for civil rights reformers to "outlaw affirmative action" and "establish the equal treatment of individuals, regardless of race, sex, or other characteristics." Among other pursuits, Rufo is a trustee of Florida's New College. Formerly, about two-thirds of New College's students were women, which Rufo called a "wildly out-of-balance student population." Yet as journalist Michelle Goldberg pointed out after speaking with Rufo, achieving gender parity isn't currently compatible with pure meritocracy, as "women are outpacing men in education." So we'd assume that Rufo would, in the name of meritocracy, be perfectly fine with men being the minority in this college. Recall that he believes "most people have a sense that different groups, different cultures, have different priorities, different interests, different talents, and they don't mathematically graft themselves in an artificial way onto every institution." We shouldn't complain about the overrepresentation of Black athletes in the NBA, the overrepresentation of Vietnamese women in nail salons, or the overrepresentation of Asian or white men in programming. So the overrepresentation of women in a college would be fine. Right?

Wrong. Rufo approvingly observes that the New College's leadership is "rebalancing the ratio of students" with the goal of achieving gender parity between men and women. If hypocrisy were an Olympic sport, Rufo would handily make off with the gold.

COMPETING FOR THE MIDDLE

We think of the DEI debate as a room with three groups standing in clusters. Proponents of the project of equality are standing on one side of the room. Opponents are standing on the opposite side. Most ordinary Americans are hanging out in the middle of the room, not paying close attention because they're getting on with their daily lives. Proponents and opponents are both trying to pull the people in the middle to their own side. Right now, opponents are trying to capture the middle by presenting themselves as advocates of colorblind equality. They're also trying to paint the proponents of equality as extremists. We shouldn't let them get away with this funhouse mirror inversion of reality.

The stakes of the DEI debate are grave. Some in the opposition have signaled that their quarrel is not just with a set of "woke" organizational practices, but rather with the entire edifice of civil rights law. Richard Hanania, whose ideas have reportedly shaped the anti-DEI policies of the second Trump administration, observes that there's a "philosophically elegant, perhaps irrefutable, libertarian case for getting rid of all anti-discrimination laws," but laments that "no matter how strong the philosophical or practical case is for doing away with anti-discrimination laws in the private sector, political reality means that they are here to stay." Influential conservative journalist Christopher Caldwell describes the Civil Rights Act of 1964 as "a legislative repeal of the First Amendment's implied right to freedom of association," and criticizes Republicans for not acknowledging "that the only way back to the free country of their ideals was through the repeal of the civil rights laws."

Proponents of equality need to help the people standing in the middle of the room understand what debate the two sides are really having underneath the rhetoric. If the debate is about the best methods of achieving a more equal society, we welcome that conversation. But if the debate is about whether it's worth striving for a more equal society in the first place, or whether civil rights laws should exist at all, we think the choice is clear. If you're in the middle of the room, we hope you think so too.

STRATEGY 1 TAKEAWAYS

- Many skeptics of DEI are reasonable, moderate people who believe in equality but have qualms about how DEI has pursued that goal. We value the opinions of this group and actively engage with their critiques.

- Many opponents, however, don't appear to believe in equality, period. Some make tortured excuses for continuing inequality. And some only seem to invoke equality when it would drive a wedge between marginalized groups or benefit dominant ones.

- Supporters of equality should relentlessly expose this second group's extremism, flimsy arguments, and hypocrisy in conversations with persuadable friends, neighbors, and colleagues.

- People in the middle deserve to know whether the DEI debate is a fight over the best methods of achieving a more equal society, or a fight over whether to strive for a more equal society in the first place.

Strategy 2:
SUPPORT DISSENT

In the 2024 presidential election, Donald Trump's MAGA movement attracted some unexpected devotees. Journalist Brock Colyar reported on young, urban professionals who'd embraced Trumpism out of disgust with "the left's puritanical obsessions with policing language and talking about identity." One voter, a college student who'd previously supported Joe Biden, explained: "I hate watching the things I say." A former Bernie Sanders supporter put it more crudely, observing that he'd switched his allegiance because he wanted the freedom to say "faggot" and "retarded."

It may be tempting to dismiss such sentiments, especially when they express a longing to use slurs. But this feeling of being suffocated by the censorious left is more common than many supporters of equality acknowledge. Like Colyar, journalist Shadi Hamid reported soon after the election that centrist and even left-leaning friends of his had become exhausted by "Democrats' cultural overreach" and expected some good to come from Trump's presidency: "I'd meet people at parties, reading groups and 'salons' who would whisper—or, when intoxicated, shout—that they could finally say what they really thought on issues such as gender identity and diversity, equity, and inclusion initiatives without fear of being ostracized."

This problem is a five-alarm fire. For too long, many advocates have acted as though supporting the equality project is self-evidently the correct choice. To draw on a colorful scenario offered by humorist David Sedaris, we behave like Americans have been given two meal options on a flight: "the chicken," or "the platter of shit with bits of broken glass in it." Unfortunately, from the perspective of many people in the middle, the decision isn't so easy. To them, the project of equality offers its own repulsive platter with bits of fanaticism, judgmentalism, and censoriousness mixed in. That's a flight where the best option is to go hungry.

To solve this problem, supporters of equality need to address two separate but related tendencies in our community: requiring strict adherence to dogma, and shaming people who depart from that dogma. Let's call these tendencies "orthodoxy."

The first tendency—requiring strict adherence to dogma—involves an intolerance for debate and disagreement. Although we hear this complaint from people across the political spectrum, conservative political commentator Ben Shapiro puts the critique most plainly: "They say 'diversity, equity, and inclusion,' and what they mean by that is 'shut up.' They don't mean inclusion, because if you have a point of view that argues with their own, then you should be quiet."

Some DEI advocates unfortunately fuel this criticism. We once delivered a presentation to a room of senior executives at a technology company. After our talk, the chief diversity officer instructed everyone in the room to share their story, one by one, of the moment they awoke to the reality of systemic racism. As we looked around, most of the executives started to squirm like they were in a dentist's chair. We can all but guarantee that some of these corporate leaders either disagreed that systemic racism existed or hadn't yet formulated a view. Nevertheless, everyone dutifully ponied up a story that would meet the specification set forth by the diversity leader.

At times the pressure to agree is even more unsparing. One of the most high-profile figures associated with the DEI movement is author and consultant Robin DiAngelo. Her blockbuster book *White Fragility* was featured on the *New York Times* bestseller list for 124 weeks. Given the influence of DiAngelo's ideas, it's striking and depressing that she puts the statement "I disagree" on a list of problematic utterances by white people in conversations about race. Every time we look at this list, we hear the thudding footfalls of Ben Shapiro taking a victory lap.

The second tendency that makes the project of equality repellent to many middle-of-the-road Americans is our propensity to shame people when they depart from the language or behavior that our dogma requires. This shaming behavior can be overt, like rebuking or insulting someone. It can also be subtle, like a condescending tone of voice, an eye-roll, or even a silent stare that makes people feel judged. One colleague of ours told us she was ready to quit her involvement in progressive advocacy groups after repeated experiences of such shaming. These included being berated for making inadvertent terminological errors, and being explicitly instructed as a white woman to say nothing in group discussions about race because her job was to "shut up and listen." "I still support progressive causes," she explained, "but these conversations make me want to take my ball and go home."

These tendencies—embracing strict dogma, and shaming people for improper language and behavior—aren't unique to the DEI community. We recognize them as a feature of many communities that hold strong moral views and feel beleaguered in their fight against the status quo, whether it's a religious sect, an animal rights organization, or an environmental group. Yet at least here in our community, orthodoxy hurts more than it helps. A more open and compassionate culture would vastly improve our ability to achieve our goals.

ORTHODOXY LEADS TO HIDDEN RESISTANCE AND FRAGILE SUPPORT

Some proponents of orthodoxy seem to think their approach will shore up support for the project of equality. But as former Georgia House Minority Leader and civic activist Stacey Abrams has stated: "If we enter this work chastising, lecturing, and hectoring, you might get a few people to do something in that moment to get you to shut up, but you're never going to convert them or convince them that it's worth doing again." Badgering someone might force them to change a policy or stop behaving a certain way. But no one is ever persuaded to change their mind by being pressured into loyalty oaths. Instead, DEI orthodoxy drives resistance underground. It leads to what economist Timur Kuran calls "preference falsification," where social pressure causes people to pretend to believe something they don't.

Preference falsification can be humiliating and alienating for the dissenter. It's also strategically harmful, as it deprives our community of an early warning system when our ideas aren't resonating. People who feel pressured into political correctness will mouth the right words in public while expressing their true views in the privacy of the voting booth. That expression of anonymous preference is much more consequential. We shouldn't have to wait every few years for election results to discover how members of the broader public really feel about our beliefs and messages. An honest conversation within our own community will give us a more realistic read.

We've repeatedly seen the benefits of such honest conversations ourselves. We're struck by the number of times we've taken a more moderate position on a DEI issue and felt relief whoosh through the room. A few years ago, local activists called for a boycott of a public school fundraiser because one of the sponsoring organizations was an evangelical church that held conservative views on LGBTQ+ issues. We felt the boycott was overkill—the church was one of many sponsors, and it wasn't publicizing any anti-LGBTQ+ viewpoints at the fundraiser. When we voiced our opinion in opposition to the boycott, a pro-DEI friend of ours let out a sigh: "Thank God you said that. I feel the same way, but was nervous about saying anything in case you agreed with the hard-line activists."

Even when people sincerely agree with you, orthodoxy can make their support fragile. Natalie Wynn, a political commentator and popular YouTuber, notes that without space for deliberation and the expression of doubts, allies can believe in progressive values only at a surface level. "It worries me, for example, if people believe 'trans women are women' because that's the slogan . . . that the smart and nice people say," says Wynn. "People who only sort of superficially understand their own political beliefs are going to be more susceptible to abandoning those beliefs at the first sign of contradiction." To riff off Wynn's example, a person who parrots the right slogans based on social pressure is more likely to crumple when reading, say, the notorious J.K. Rowling essay that opposes trans rights. By contrast, a person who has worked through their doubts about trans issues with a thoughtful and patient interlocutor will likely be less fazed.

ORTHODOXY CREATES A SMALL TENT

Orthodoxy can also mask a deep hopelessness about a society's capacity for reform, which can then become a self-fulfilling prophecy. As columnist Michelle Goldberg argues, progressives often show "contempt" for persuasion, based on the view that if someone is "turned off by my rhetorical style, then they were already a sexist or a racist." Journalist Anand Giridharadas also critiques the progressive tendency to assume "that differences of identity are unbridgeable, that people are too invested in their privileges and interests to change."

It's true that social justice supporters often articulate how painful they find it to engage in dialogue with people who hold different viewpoints. This can be particularly so when the conversation touches on their core identity. We often hear versions of the line: "I shouldn't have to debate my equal humanity." As gay men, we certainly dreaded debating same-sex marriage in the late 2000s and early 2010s, given that we viewed marriage equality as a matter of basic respect for the equal humanity of ourselves and our families. Yet our community had no alternative but to engage in those debates if we hoped to make social progress. Refusing to debate our equal humanity in cases like these means our opponents win by default.

On purely strategic terms, refusing to engage is a dangerous battle plan when supporters of the equality project are the ones with less political, legal, and cultural power. Consider the findings of a 2018 Hidden Tribes of America survey of more than eight thousand respondents. The survey found only 8 percent of Americans were "progressive activists," meaning those who deeply care about "issues concerning equity, fairness, and America's direction today," and who tend to be secular and cosmopolitan. A further 11 percent were "traditional liberals" who value tolerance and compromise, and who put faith in institutions. We won't win the culture by insisting that everybody squeeze into one of these two buckets, which together amount to less than one fifth of the population. To build a sustainable majority, the cause of equality must find support from other categories identified in the Hidden Tribes survey. That includes passive liberals (15 percent), politically disengaged voters (26 percent), moderates (15 percent), and perhaps even some traditional conservatives (19 percent). We ourselves have found that many moderate and center-right voters can be champions of equality efforts so long as they're not expected to endorse the entire checklist of progressive causes. And in case you're wondering whether the political landscape has shifted dramatically since 2018, another set of polls in 2025 found that only 13 percent of Americans hold "strong liberal" views, while 46 percent consider themselves "moderate," "somewhat conservative," or "somewhat liberal."

Representative Sarah McBride, the first openly transgender member of the United States Congress, similarly argues that to advance trans rights, supporters need to "create space for some imperfect allies." She elaborates that getting to a slight majority in support of "basic nondiscrimination protections" and "protecting access to medically necessary care" for trans people will, by definition, require supporters to include "some people in the seventy percent who oppose trans people participating in sports." For McBride, the conversation about sports access "needs to continue with people, but we can't dismiss them as bigots or remove them from our coalition, because then we will have a ceiling of thirty percent on any coalition in defense of anyone's rights."

This point transcends current debates about gender identity. Many—perhaps most—Americans are neither passionate supporters of social justice nor hardline opponents. They believe in treating people with fairness and respect but may have doubts about DEI or be unaware of the latest terminology. Proponents of the equality project should be listening to, and engaging with, people in this middle group, not making them fearful to express their perspectives.

ORTHODOXY MAKES THE EQUALITY PROJECT LOOK FOOLISH

Orthodoxy also makes our cause seem fringe in several ways. First, it can pressure people to embrace the furthest left position. Our community is generally made up of idealistic people with a strong moral commitment to challenging power structures such as white supremacy and patriarchy. In such a community, no one wants to be out-PCed, because disagreeing with the most progressive members of the community feels like letting the cause down. But it lets the cause down even more to stay silent.

In a conversation with a room full of civil rights leaders, we brought up one of the most infamous, and influential, papers associated with the field of DEI—a short document written by DEI facilitator Tema Okun called "White Supremacy Culture." The paper lists "characteristics of white supremacy culture which show up in our organizations," including "perfectionism," a "sense of urgency," "worship of the written word," and "objectivity," among many others. The paper offers barely any citations for its claims, let alone analysis connecting the listed values to white supremacy. Yet it spread like wildfire in progressive and nonprofit circles, and is sometimes deployed to challenge the legitimacy of standard workplace practices like deadlines and project management.

We mentioned to the room that while we've always disagreed with the arguments in this paper, we've been historically reluctant to speak up when a colleague invokes it, as it could be taken as evidence that we're insufficiently committed to eradicating white supremacy in all its forms. One leader in the room, a Black man, erupted. He denounced the paper and pushed us and others to do the same. When we allow silly ideas to proliferate without objection, he said, it discredits the cause and undermines our ability to address the genuine forms of white supremacy that continue to need urgent attention.

Engineering professor Chris Cooper adds another downside of allowing the furthest left positions to be aired without dissent: it gives a misleading impression of the DEI community to observers. In our experience, the median member of the community is thoughtful and balanced. Yet as Cooper points out, the general public and politicians form "their opinions of DEI based on the voices of those with the megaphones," even if the people with the megaphones aren't remotely representative.

Another way orthodoxy makes our cause seem foolish is persnickety language-policing. We were once in a room of twenty leaders for a roundtable to discuss advancing racial equality in their industry. Some participants expressed consternation about the underrepresentation of "Latinx" individuals and asked to explore how to boost their numbers. Yet the mere mention of the word "Latinx"—a gender-neutral alternative to "Latino" and "Latina"—ignited a tinderbox. Some individuals strenuously objected to the use of "Latinx," arguing that the term was a colonialist invention that didn't make sense in the Spanish language. Others defended the label, noting that the common use of "Latino" as a collective noun erased the existence of women and that "Latinx" was more inclusive of all genders. We tried to steer the conversation back to the substantive problem we were trying to solve—the underrepresentation of Latino (or Latinx!) individuals in the industry—but the participants in the conversation would have none of it. "Words matter," one intoned. The continued debate about terminology kept us from discussing anything else.

We're the last people to deny that words matter. Our previous book was devoted to the topic of inclusive communication. Yet we find in conversations about equality that emphasis on proper language can sometimes rise to the level of absurdity. Consider the widely pilloried "Elimination of Harmful Language Initiative" at Stanford University, a thirteen-page document listing the dos and don'ts of inclusive language. The guide recommended retiring the term "user" when describing people who utilize software or services, due to its negative associations with "those who suffer from substance abuse issues." It also criticized "white paper" for assigning "value connotations" to being white, and "war room" for its "unnecessary use of violent language." These complicated rules of acceptable and unacceptable language do little to address injustice. But they do a lot to make the project of equality seem fussy and trivial.

ORTHODOXY LETS OPPONENTS OFF THE HOOK

A final cost of orthodoxy is that it makes it harder to resist the suppression of speech on the other side. This is a dire concession. Opponents of DEI are banning books from libraries, dictating what teachers can talk about in their classrooms, restricting the content of employer training programs, cracking down on protestors, threatening and suing media companies, and purging language they don't like from government websites. We should be on the front foot with a vigorous defense of free speech. Yet our own climate of conformity and self-censorship opens us to charges of hypocrisy when we condemn such behavior.

Free speech principles are also essential for legal reasons, as they offer the strongest shield for equality work in this brutal legal environment. In 2022, the Florida legislature enacted the "Stop W.O.K.E. Act," which muzzled schools and employers from teaching certain concepts relating to race, gender, and other diversity issues. A federal court struck down a provision of the law relating to workplace training, finding that it likely violated the free speech clause of the First Amendment. The appeals court observed: "Florida may be exactly right about the nature of the ideas it targets. Or it may not. Either way, the merits of these views will be decided in the clanging marketplace of ideas rather than a codebook or a courtroom."

Free speech arguments similarly persuaded a federal judge to block an executive order in Donald Trump's first term that tried to regulate which forms of diversity training private entities could conduct. Perhaps in response to that smackdown, the Trump administration did a hard pivot when it released a similar executive order in the second term. While the second order aims to crush "illegal DEI" throughout the public and private sectors, it also contains an explicit carve-out allowing organizations to engage in pro-DEI "First Amendment-protected speech." Presumably, the administration realized that going after speech would lead to a judicial drubbing. And while the conservative justices on the current Supreme Court have been hostile to pure equality arguments, they've lauded free speech in opinion after opinion. Defenses of equality grounded in speech principles may have the best chance of victory at the current court.

In short, our ability to promote and defend equality initiatives will depend on muscular protections for free speech. Supporters of equality can't embrace the value of free speech when it favors us but reject it when doubters wish to speak.

EMBRACE FREE SPEECH AND PARTIAL PERSUASION

How, then, can supporters of the equality project welcome dissent?

We can start by explicitly embracing free speech as a core value of the project of equality. We agree with human rights advocate Suzanne Nossel, who writes in her book *Dare to Speak* that "concerns of diversity and inclusion can—and must—be reconciled with robust protections for speech." These values are often pitted against each other. Those who care about diversity and inclusion worry about how speech can harm members of marginalized groups. Those who care about free speech worry about how norms of diversity and inclusion can stifle authentic self-expression. Yet speech and equality often don't clash and can even be mutually reinforcing. As Nossel points out, trying to speak inclusively, such as by avoiding stereotypes and not denigrating others, makes it easier for people to join in conversation who otherwise feel shut down. Strong protections for free speech also enable communities on the margins of society to make claims on the majority without being punished. This marriage between equality and free speech needs to become a rallying cry for the new era of equality work.

Next, equality advocates need to create room for allies and doubters to work through their concerns. In practice, this means the words "I disagree" are perfectly acceptable to utter in conversations about equality issues, so long as disagreements are handled respectfully. Welcoming a variety of perspectives means equality advocates will need to tolerate opinions that make some of us wince, such as views defending traditional conceptions of gender and sexuality. You don't need to agree with everything you hear, or sit in silence and nod along. But your conversation partner won't be convinced by your point of view if their own perspectives, fears, or doubts are being quashed.

Finally, look for what marketing professor Jonah Berger calls a person's "zone of acceptance." A zone of acceptance refers to the range of viewpoints that someone could potentially support. A person whose politics are center-left might be persuaded of ideas within a zone ranging from the progressive left to the center-right. Someone on the far right might be persuaded by ideas ranging from where they already are to the center-right. Anything outside of that zone is what Berger calls the "region of rejection"—the viewpoints so far away from a person's starting point that the individual is unalterably opposed to them.

Try to persuade someone of a viewpoint within their region of rejection and it's likely to backfire, causing them to double down on their initial position. A business leader may be open to the idea that diversity initiatives are helpful to the company's bottom line, but not to the idea that a commitment to diversity requires ending capitalism. A social conservative may be open to the view that LGBTQ+ customers should be protected against discrimination, but not that religious vendors should be required to cater same-sex weddings. While looking for an ideological opponent's "zone of acceptance" can require restraints of tongue and pen, the payoff of persistence can be tremendous. A person you convince by patiently stepping through arguments they can reasonably accept will become a much deeper ally than someone you convince with boilerplate slogans.

MOVE FROM ONE TYPE OF JUDGMENT TO ANOTHER

Even if our community tolerates a wider range of opinions, people will still cross the line by speaking and acting non-inclusively. Here, supporters of equality must tread carefully. Instead of rendering "judgment" in the sense of chastising people for errors, we recommend exercising a different form of "judgment" in the sense of discernment. Specifically, our community needs the judgment to choose among three responses: condemnation, coaching, and circumspection.

When someone's behavior is egregious, or they've repeatedly shown they're uninterested in learning how to treat others with basic respect, go ahead and condemn—we don't lose sleep over the plight of Harvey Weinstein. But if all you have is the elephant gun of shaming and ostracism, you're going to blow away a lot of mice. You'll also create a circular firing squad, given that no one is infallible in these conversations. We, regrettably, have confused students of the same ethnicity with each other, used the wrong pronouns to refer to transgender colleagues, and laughed at demeaning jokes. If everyone who makes a misstep risks punishment, and everyone makes missteps, then it logically follows that all of us should live in a state of perpetual dread. Most people can only tolerate such a state for so long.

That's why, in ordinary situations of non-inclusive behavior, we recommend coaching instead of condemnation. This approach replaces the attitude of a scold with the attitude of a mentor who's there to help the other person learn from mistakes. Coaching surrenders none of the core ideals of inclusion. It remains rock-ribbed in seeking to transform the status quo and to push people toward higher standards of conduct. It differs only—but critically—in the means it adopts to pursue those ends.

Most importantly, coaching doesn't display a uniformly punitive attitude to errors. In the vast run of cases, a coach adopts a rehabilitative mindset, treating people as more than the mistakes they've made. Instead of shaming someone for an off-putting joke, a coach would say something like: "You're a kind and caring person, so what you said surprised me. Can you explain or rephrase?" As psychologist Scott Plous observes, affirming the person but challenging the conduct primes their "egalitarian self-image." This, in turn, often causes them to resolve the conflict between the person you praised and the conduct you challenged by bringing their behavior into alignment with who they are.

Coaching also offers practical tools. To improve, it's not enough for people to know their behavior was wrong. They also need to know what made it unacceptable, what behavior to adopt instead, and how to cultivate the skills to get better. A coach sees the task of navigating a rapidly changing social landscape as eminently teachable, much like learning a new language. While often seeming mysterious, the skills needed to have effective conversations about identity are tangible. As we discussed in our last book, we can all learn how to build resilience and curiosity, how to apologize authentically and disagree respectfully, and how to support targets of bias. A coach spends vastly more time helping the learner acquire such competencies than they do pointing out the learner's shortcomings.

Unlike an approach that leans into shaming and blaming, coaching is effective because it doesn't shut people down. In our experience, the people most attracted to the "condemnation" approach are drawn to it for valid reasons—it seems to create accountability where other methods have failed. Yet the irony is that by seeking to create accountability through the raw exercise of power, condemnation makes the learner resentful and resistant to change. By adopting a more compassionate approach, coaching is more likely to lead the other person to take true responsibility.

We've mentioned when the right strategy is condemnation and when it's coaching. The final approach, "circumspection," is reserved for situations where the proper response is simply to let it go. We've been in multiple conversations where well-meaning older colleagues use the term "sexual preference" to describe sexual orientation. Within the LGBTQ+ community today, "sexual preference" is widely disfavored for its implicit suggestion that a person's sexuality is a choice. But we try not to get too wound up when a well-meaning person who grew up with this term continues to use it. Not every infraction needs to be pointed out, just like not every jaywalker needs to be fined.

In other words, sometimes even coaching is an excessive response. Our guideposts are to weigh the importance of the issue, the apparent intentions of the speaker, and whether the offending person is likely to receive our feedback as helpful or irritating. When an issue is small, the other person appears to have no malicious intent, and correcting them would make us seem meddlesome, we refrain. The decision to let it go doesn't mean we aren't committed to advancing inclusion any more than a spouse who refrains from correcting every slight isn't committed to a respectful marriage. But in both cases, part of being in relationship with others means allowing them to be imperfect, as we are ourselves.

SUPPORTING DISSENT WILL HELP EQUALITY WIN

Some people who criticize a culture of orthodoxy in the DEI movement do so for nakedly political reasons. They want to paint DEI supporters in the worst possible light so people will join the opposition, yet they conveniently ignore the insularity and judgmentalism on their own side. As we've already established, opponents of the equality project have their own rigid ideologies and their own objects of scorn—people of color they judge to be low IQ, women they judge to be selfish, LGBTQ+ individuals they judge to be morally depraved.

We're acutely aware of the dangers of piling on with a similar critique to those that have been voiced for years by anti-DEI ideologues. Yet it's precisely because we're so passionate about, and personally invested in, the values of inclusion and equality that we want this work to win the support of the American people. Imposing ideological purity tests and sneering at transgressors may help us feel morally righteous, but it does little to help the marginalized people who need our movement to be strong. Ours shouldn't be the side that's perceived by ordinary Americans as stifling and sanctimonious. It should be the side that gives people the freedom to speak, the space to doubt, and the grace to make mistakes.

STRATEGY 2 TAKEAWAYS

- The project of equality has a reputation for requiring strict adherence to dogma, and for shaming people who depart from that dogma.

- This behavior causes people to hide their true viewpoints, makes the support of allies more fragile, limits the size of the pro-equality coalition, makes the project of equality seem foolish, and makes it harder to call out opponents' infringements of free speech.

- Supporters of equality should embrace free speech as a core value, and welcome dissent.

- Supporters should move from condemnation to coaching, and sometimes even from coaching to circumspection.

Strategy 3:
WELCOME NEW GROUPS

When we taught our first class on diversity and inclusion, we asked our students to draw three concentric circles. In the innermost circle, we told them to write down the social groups within the "core" of DEI. In the next circle out, we told them to write "secondary" groups that should be included in the DEI conversation but were less central to the project. Finally, in the outer ring, we told students to list groups that fell outside DEI discourse altogether.

Students found the "core" groups easy to identify. These groups tracked the classifications protected by civil rights laws, such as race, ethnicity, gender, sexual orientation, gender identity, and disability. But once we moved beyond the inner circle, the consensus collapsed. What about people of low socioeconomic status, veterans, first-gen individuals (those who are the first in their family to attend college), introverts, obese people, vegans and vegetarians, anti-vaxxers, left-handed people, unattractive people, or people from rural areas? These other groups aren't protected by the law, but they often experience bias or exclusion from mainstream institutions. Should the project of equality care about these groups? If so, why? If not, why not?

Students swiftly realized it was impossible to do equality work without making tough calls about which groups most deserve support. Although DEI experts often rail against a "hierarchy of oppression," some kind of hierarchy is inevitable. Questions of value aside, resources are limited. The project of equality can't possibly encompass every group in society, and if it tried, it would become scattered and ineffective.

Traditionally, DEI advocates have solved this challenge by prioritizing the core groups protected by anti-discrimination laws. Even then, some core groups have risen to the top of the pile. If you go to a diversity training session, read a book on DEI, attend diversity conferences, or review the inclusion initiatives offered by major companies and universities, race and gender are usually central. After people of color and women, the second tier of core groups include the LGBTQ+ community and, to a lesser extent, the disability community. Most practitioners will tell you with utmost sincerity that their work is intended to create an inclusive environment for people of *all* identities and backgrounds. But in practice, beyond these groups, the field has given the claims of other cohorts short shrift.

We're troubled by this narrow approach. While it's impossible for the project of equality to include everyone on earth, focusing only on the "core" DEI cohorts overlooks other important forms of social disadvantage, breeding resentment among the communities that miss out. Nowadays, at least three such communities are making forceful claims that deserve the attention of equality advocates. The first group consists of people who are already protected by civil rights law, but argue that DEI hasn't adequately enforced their issues. We call these "claims of enforcement." The second group comprises people in dominant social groups who say their own vulnerabilities have been ignored. We call these "claims of symmetry." The third group consists of people who aren't protected by civil rights law at all, but nonetheless want to be included in the project of equality. We call these "claims of extension."

The project of equality will drive itself into oblivion if it's too slow or too rigid to recognize contemporary forms of inequality. Instead of limiting ourselves to traditional identity groups, equality advocates should respond as a superhero would and go where the pain is. It's time to listen to claims of enforcement, symmetry, and extension with an open heart and an open mind.

CLAIMS OF ENFORCEMENT

Some cohorts are already protected by law but feel that DEI has neglected them. Disability and age are common examples. Congress passed landmark legislation protecting disabled individuals from discrimination in 1973 and 1990. Nevertheless, decades later, disability advocates often argue their issues have been devalued in DEI conversations. Congress enacted age discrimination legislation even earlier—in 1967. Here too advocates argue that while ageism is rife, DEI efforts do little to combat it.

The claim of enforcement we hear most these days, however, is religion. American law gives religion pride of place, protecting the free exercise of religion in the First Amendment to the U.S. Constitution. Religion is also one of only five classifications explicitly protected under the Civil Rights Act of 1964. People of faith have repeatedly won at the Supreme Court when they bring discrimination claims or request accommodations, including Jehovah's Witnesses who don't wish to salute the flag or cite the Pledge of Allegiance, Amish families who object to compulsory education, and Christian employees who seek not to work on the Sabbath. Yet while the law cherishes religion, the field of DEI frequently treats it as an afterthought.

Eboo Patel, the founder and president of Interfaith America, believes the "worldviews of people in DEI spaces" have tended to accord less importance to religion than other topics. Patel's colleague, Megan Johnson, observes: "We're often approached by diversity professionals who are really versed in race, gender, sexuality, and they're like, 'Oh, I don't get religion, and I'm not comfortable with it.'" We're not entirely sure why this discomfort exists, but we have some guesses. In our experience, the vast majority of diversity professionals have college degrees, and polling data shows that college graduates are less likely than non-college-educated Americans to say religion is important in their lives. They're also less likely to pray on a daily basis, and more likely to describe themselves as atheists or agnostics. Diversity leaders may also think it's easier to create a figurative wall between religion and work to avoid conflicts between conservative religious communities and LGBTQ+ communities.

Yet it's self-destructive to sideline a form of identity that nearly half of Americans (45 percent) describe as "very important" to them. The United States has a high level of religious diversity and is the most devout country in the Western world. Given these realities, the field needs to show it respects religious believers and cares about their ability to authentically practice their faith. And it must give secular and religious people tools to build meaningful and empathetic relationships despite their different worldviews.

Over the years, people from many different faith backgrounds have expressed frustration at DEI's inattention to their needs. Muslim scholar Nadia Ahmad argues that "even in spaces that champion diversity and inclusion, Muslim voices remain expendable" and that mainstream diversity programs "fail to address" the daily bias that she and other Muslims experience. Evelyn Alsultany, author of *Broken: The Failed Promise of Muslim Inclusion*, observes that Muslim identity tends to get included in DEI initiatives in response to momentary crises that bring public attention to Islamophobia, like the backlash to the plan for a Muslim community center to be built near the former World Trade Center site in Manhattan. Yet she argues that DEI ignores the deeper structural causes of Islamophobia, like national security policies that demonize Muslims. Organizations can also ignore the needs of Muslims by not recognizing their holidays (such as Eid), not respecting their prayer obligations, or structuring social activities around consumption of alcohol.

Some of the most recent and prominent claims of enforcement have come from the Jewish community. Whether Jewish identity is conceptualized primarily as a religion, a culture, an ancestry, or all three, the Jewish community clearly deserves to be included in the project of equality. A Jewish person faces more than double the risk of being a victim of a hate crime than any other demographic group in the United States. Antisemitic hate speech is surging online. Synagogues are being vandalized with Nazi symbols. In a 2024 survey of nearly two thousand American Jews, one third of respondents said they'd been personally targeted by antisemitism at least once over the prior year, and more than a quarter of American Jewish college students said they'd felt uncomfortable or unsafe at a campus event because of their Jewish identity. Yet Jewish DEI advocate Debbie Epstein Henry speaks for many when she laments that Jews "have not been welcome" under the DEI umbrella. Her explanations for this omission include that "some believe Jews are not marginalized" but rather are "white and part of a dominant majority and don't need protection."

It's one thing to argue that DEI has done a poor job responding to antisemitism. What makes us tear our hair out is the assertion—often made by members of the Trump administration—that organizations should simultaneously abandon DEI and focus on fixing antisemitism. That's like saying hospitals should ditch cancer research and focus on curing leukemia. Even assuming the administration is sincerely committed to stamping out antisemitism, it would be more logical to consider those efforts an *expansion* of DEI. Tackling deep-seated forms of bias and discrimination against minority groups is literally what the field of DEI was established to do.

Thankfully, the project of equality has already started increasing its focus on religion. In recent years, many large corporations have launched faith-based or interfaith affinity groups for employees, or otherwise incorporated religion into diversity conversations. This work should continue as the field strives to better reflect the diversity of the nation it serves.

CLAIMS OF SYMMETRY

Sometimes, the people seeking inclusion in the DEI tent are making claims of symmetry—they argue the field's concern for people on the "non-dominant" side of a demographic divide has obscured the needs of people on the "dominant" side. Specifically, they argue that groups cast as dominant can have their own vulnerabilities.

It's critical to exercise caution in this context. When a dominant group claims to be vulnerable, we must distinguish between the pain of losing dominant-group status and genuine forms of pain that require our attention. Let us be clear: the pain of having to share space with other groups, or the pain of having to compete with people on a level playing field, is not a legitimate grievance.

In that regard, many claims of symmetry are absurd on their face. Consider philosopher Paul Gottfried's statement that "the systematic degradation of white Americans" is "infinitely more frightening" than segregation. Huh? But claims of symmetry may be valid in specific and narrow settings. For instance, while we'd never suggest heterosexual people are disadvantaged as a class, we recall a conversation with a diversity leader at a theatrical organization who told us that gay men had come to dominate some segments of the organization, and were acting in ways that caused the straight minority to feel excluded and demeaned. Again, it's important to consider such claims with caution—dominant groups aren't accustomed to being in the minority, and merely feeling uncomfortable isn't itself a form of marginalization. But we see no reason to dismiss these claims out of hand. The project of equality should absolutely protect straight people against discriminatory treatment by a local gay majority in the rare situations where such treatment arises.

To us, the most prominent example of a legitimate claim of symmetry relates to gender. Richard Reeves, a senior fellow at the Brookings Institution, is the author of the book *Of Boys and Men*. In that work, he argues that while men continue to dominate the white-collar professional world in areas like politics, business, and law, they now experience disadvantages in schooling and the non-elite labor force. Boys are more likely than girls to fail key school subjects (math, reading, and science); are less likely to graduate high school; and are further behind women in college degree attainment than women were behind men in the 1970s. Over the past few decades, men's labor force participation has declined, and traditionally male jobs have been disproportionately hit by automation and free trade. Men are also more likely to live with their parents into their late twenties and early thirties, engage in alcohol or drug abuse, experience homelessness, and die by suicide.

Reeves doesn't argue a focus on the plight of men should replace feminist efforts to advance girls and women. Nor could he: women continue to face severe disadvantages like the gender pay gap, domestic violence, sexual harassment and abuse, a heavier burden of unpaid care work and housework, greater risk of poverty, attacks on their reproductive autonomy, and significant underrepresentation in corporate and political leadership. Instead, he argues gender inequality shouldn't be treated "as a one-way street." Societies, he contends, should tackle disadvantages in both directions, such as by encouraging more men to enter fields traditionally dominated by women like health, education, administration, and literacy (HEAL), just as we try to incorporate more women into science, technology, engineering, and mathematics

STRATEGY 3: WELCOME NEW GROUPS

(STEM). In an educational setting, other researchers have suggested efforts to boost outcomes for boys, such as adding more hands-on interactive activities into lesson plans, building more breaks into the school day, finding ways to increase men's representation in the K-12 teaching profession, and using a more "relational" pedagogical method that emphasizes building positive relationships between teachers and students.

Historically, the field of DEI has largely ignored issues relating to men. When we told a room of diversity professionals that we wanted the field to pay greater attention to this topic, a male diversity practitioner immediately rejected the idea: "This is just men complaining that women are finally becoming more equal to them." Afterward, another male diversity practitioner told us he sympathized with us in that moment, because he too had found it challenging to broach these issues: "On more than one occasion, I have brought up the suicide, depression, and financial pressures faced by men and the achievement gaps we are seeing with boys. Unfortunately, this has often been met with eye-rolls, dismissals, or awkward stares from members of the DEI community." He added: "One person laughed and said, 'What are you—a men's rights activist?' Another told me they just could not bring themselves to care about men."

We believe this attitude is a big mistake. At countless events about diversity, we've heard the plaintive refrain: "Why are hardly any men here?" One likely answer is that men don't see themselves in this work. They're lionized as the people who are supposed to solve all the organization's diversity problems, or demonized as the cause of those problems, but in either case they're on the outside looking in. Yet men are also harmed by patriarchal norms. One survey of frontline workers by gender equality organization Catalyst found that 75 percent of men feel they must sacrifice their authenticity when they're expected to be aggressive, independent, and competitive at work, and 87 percent of men want it to be more acceptable for them to express traits like empathy and kindness. Any diversity program that discusses the harm of gender stereotypes could easily incorporate these topics.

Catalyst CEO Jennifer McCollum shared with us that when she used to give talks only about women's unique challenges and disadvantages, women (but not men) would come up to her afterward to share their stories and seek advice. Now that she also discusses barriers faced by men, the dynamics in the room have completely shifted. People of all genders swarm her after her talks to engage in deeper conversation and to thank her for seeing their struggles. Including men in the tent is an opportunity to reinvigorate the project of equality by engaging huge swaths of people who have been sitting on the sidelines.

CLAIMS OF EXTENSION

Finally, some groups who seek to be included in the project of equality aren't currently protected by law at all. Perhaps the most obvious candidate here is social class.

On any number of measures, working-class individuals are disadvantaged relative to college-educated professionals. Americans without a college degree are more likely than college graduates to be arrested or incarcerated, to be diagnosed with mental illness, to suffer chronic pain, and to experience "deaths of despair" from drug abuse, alcohol, or suicide. Their life expectancy is lower. They're also less likely to get married, to have close friends, to report life satisfaction, and to secure a well-paid job. As the American economy has shifted away from industries like manufacturing toward service and knowledge jobs, working-class Americans have faced stagnant wages while college graduates continue to climb the economic ladder.

Even when Americans from working-class backgrounds seek to access a college education or white-collar jobs, they confront a steeplechase of obstacles. Parental income almost perfectly predicts a child's chances of going to college. Many elite colleges have more students in the top 1 percent of the income scale than the entire bottom 60 percent. And even for those who push past those obstacles and obtain higher degrees, the struggle continues. People from lower socioeconomic backgrounds are substantially less likely to become managers than their peers from higher ones—a phenomenon dubbed the "class ceiling." For those who seek employment in the elite jobs of law, consulting, or investment banking, research shows such firms systematically screen out candidates from lower socioeconomic backgrounds to find those with the right "pedigree."

Americans from working-class backgrounds are also barely represented in the halls of power. College graduates represent a whopping 96 percent of members of the House of Representatives, even though less than 40 percent of the adult population has a college degree. While less than 10 percent of the American population are millionaires, more than half of Congressmembers are. To restore public trust in our democracy, these stark disparities need urgent correction.

The field of DEI has traditionally neglected people from lower socioeconomic backgrounds in a couple of ways. First, it has often failed to analyze social class as its own distinct form of disadvantage. Organizations don't typically mention social class or socioeconomic status in their diversity statements, representation goals, demographic reporting, or diversity programs. If they do, class is mentioned significantly less often than other identity characteristics.

Compounding these issues, the DEI conversation itself has tended to occur much more within the professional managerial class than within the working class. It's a testament to DEI's success as a field that it became embedded in America's most elite institutions, including Fortune 500 companies, major professional services firms, selective colleges, and private schools. But this success has meant conversations about the project of equality are happening more among people who've already attained a degree of economic privilege. We're much more regularly asked to present on diversity issues to investment bankers and software engineers than we're asked to present to retail clerks or construction workers. This class distinction also holds within organizations: in our experience, many law firms make diversity programs available to lawyers while excluding business professionals like administrative assistants.

All these dynamics have made it easy for opponents to paint the field as "elite," "establishment," and "out of touch." They've also allowed a false narrative to flourish: the idea that efforts to advance equality for people of color, women, and LGBTQ+ individuals are forms of non-economic "identity politics" that conflict with the interests and values of working people. Is it any wonder that white working-class Americans have increasingly come to feel resentful toward DEI?

It's not just the populist right, but also the populist left that has argued the correct response to this working-class angst is to ditch DEI. Faiz Shakir, a political advisor to Senator Bernie Sanders, argues that DEI programs "soften the actual confrontation with corporate power we need in society." Jennifer C. Pan, author of *Selling Social Justice*, argues DEI is "fundamentally a tool of management," deployed to undermine union campaigns. In this telling, the field's neglect of social class is intentional; it focuses on "identity" issues like race, gender, and sexual orientation to distract and divide the working class.

We disagree. Many canonical race- and gender-based initiatives are fundamentally economic, aimed at closing the racial wealth gap, gender pay gap, and other economic disparities that affect working-class women and people of color. It's also highly unlikely that if corporate leaders spurned the project of equality, they'd suddenly face increased pressure to unionize their workforces and lift the pay of low-wage employees. The way forward is not to ditch the equality project, but rather to draw social class into its values and practices.

The work of equality must explicitly aim to increase socioeconomic diversity and inclusion in institutions like universities and workplaces. This could involve reducing or eliminating college admissions practices that give preference to children of alumni or donors, engaging in class-based affirmative action, recruiting from a wider range of colleges with socioeconomically diverse student pools, removing unnecessary degree requirements from job postings, adopting a more cooperative rather than combative approach to unions, incorporating class issues into diversity workshops and presentations, offering leadership and development training programs specifically for "first-gen" professionals, and auditing recruitment and promotion practices for implicit biases that screen out candidates from lower socioeconomic backgrounds. Given that the "diploma divide" between college-educated Americans and working-class Americans is one of the biggest drivers of this country's political polarization, a greater focus on social class could do a lot to reverse the anti-DEI backlash.

Class isn't the only viable claim of extension. Another is a claim made by conservatives in academia, who correctly point out that most universities are dominated by liberals. Columnist Megan McArdle argues that the problem of academia being "near-monolithically left" can't be solved simply by addressing overt bias or demanding that universities hire more conservatives. She observes that progressives will often look for "reasons to blackball" conservative candidates. Moreover, even where there's no explicit discrimination, "there are subtler ways that majority groups inadvertently exclude minorities." Conservatives will be "held to a higher standard" because "a thousand objections will flood the minds of left-leaning colleagues." And "they'll need to be extra charming to overcome the fact that they won't naturally come across as 'one of us.'" In short, McArdle concludes we'll "need something much more ambitious to overcome those human realities—something, in fact, that looks similar to what we call DEI."

As a general matter, conservatives aren't a marginalized group. They are, in fact, in charge of many of our society's ruling institutions. Yet as we discussed in the case of men and boys, a group can be generally dominant but worthy of support in certain important pockets of society. In academia, we agree with McArdle that conservatives are at a disadvantage in faculty hiring across many disciplines, and we believe institutions of higher learning should do more to recruit and welcome conservative voices on campus. An intellectual monoculture isn't healthy for truth-seeking or for preserving the legitimacy of higher education in our ideologically diverse nation.

THE LEGAL INCENTIVE TO WELCOME NEW GROUPS

So far we've urged the project of equality to welcome new groups for social and political reasons. The imperative to consider new groups also arises out of legal necessity. As we've noted, the Supreme Court clearly signaled in its 2023 *Students for Fair Admissions* decision that it holds a "colorblind" or identity-neutral view of civil rights law. This means it's now significantly riskier for organizations to adopt programs that give preference to individuals based on characteristics protected by law (like race or sex), even if those preferences are well-meaning attempts to uplift marginalized groups. An organization can't engage in affirmative action for people of color because "race" is a protected category, but it can engage in affirmative action for groups like veterans, people from lower socioeconomic backgrounds, and individuals without college degrees, because those groups aren't protected by law.

Given the overlap between race and socioeconomic status, many equality advocates have noticed that a focus on socioeconomic status could help advance racial diversity goals. Here we offer a word of warning. Any organization that picks another identity as a proxy for race may face legal challenges arguing its efforts are a pretext for race discrimination.

Consider the case of Thomas Jefferson High School of Science and Technology. This public magnet school in Virginia had an admissions policy that didn't take race into account, but instead considered socioeconomic factors like geographic diversity and eligibility for free or reduced-price meals. A group of parents and alums filed a lawsuit alleging that while this policy didn't mention race, the intention behind it was to reduce the number of Asian Americans admitted. The lower court agreed with the parents, while the appeals court ruled for the school. Then the Supreme Court refused to hear a further appeal, leaving the school's policy in place. Justice Alito wrote a scathing dissent, lambasting the decision not to hear the case. He called the appeals court decision in favor of the school "flagrantly wrong," adding that the school's policy was being "trumpeted" as a "blueprint" for evading the Supreme Court's ruling in the *Students for Fair Admissions* decision. Only time will tell whether Justice Alito, here joined only by Justice Thomas, will persuade a majority of the court to agree with him. We believe policies like the one at this high school are legally permissible. But it's safest for educational institutions and workplaces that want to advance socioeconomic diversity to do so for its own sake, rather than to skirt prohibitions on race-based affirmative action.

Another legal loophole relates to programs for older individuals and disabled individuals. Both groups are legally protected, but under different laws than the one that prohibits race and sex discrimination. The laws relating to age and disability don't allow "reverse" discrimination claims, meaning a younger person or non-disabled person can't claim they were discriminated against based on their youth or lack of disability. This restriction is hugely significant. It means organizations have wide latitude to engage in affirmative action practices that favor older people or disabled people without having to worry about getting sued as they would when pursuing affirmative action favoring people of color or women. Organizations can, for instance, give disabled students more time to complete tests, give preference to disabled employees in hiring and promotion, or provide special training opportunities for older workers.

THE DILUTION CRITIQUE

By this point you might be wondering why on earth the project of equality *wouldn't* welcome new groups. The most common explanation we hear from equality advocates is that such expansion would dilute the attention given to currently recognized groups. If the field opens its arms to religious people, disaffected men, and working-class individuals, and leans more heavily into programs based on age, disability, veteran status, and other characteristics, some fear it could blur the project's long-standing focus on people of color and women.

This fear has some empirical basis. In one study, researchers examined diversity statements on law firm websites spanning a decade (2010–2019) and compared the statements against the firms' demographic data. Over that period, firms tended to broaden their definitions of diversity to include not just legally protected categories like race and gender, but also perspectives, backgrounds, and experiences. The researchers found that "as definitions of diversity broadened, fewer racial minorities were hired." (The same effect didn't apply to gender.) While careful not to directly attribute reductions in hiring of people of color to the diversity statements, the researchers nonetheless considered it "suggestive evidence that a more 'inclusive' definition of diversity" was "associated with firms having relatively fewer racial minority employees."

Aside from the empirical concern, welcoming new groups raises a conceptual challenge. An openness to new claims by previously unrecognized social groups could unleash what Kenji has previously described as "pluralism anxiety"—the fear of the possibly endless parade of balkanized cohorts all vying for recognition. How is the project of equality supposed to adjudicate among competing claims of disadvantage from men and women, the white working class and Black professionals, Israeli Jews and Arab Muslims, Christian conservatives and the LGBTQ+ community? The potential for the "oppression Olympics" is real, which could make the overall project of equality weaker and messier.

Despite these challenges, the dilution critique shouldn't deter the field from a more expansive understanding of who's included. Had society refused to expand the project of equality until the nation had fully atoned for its original sins of slavery and colonialism, the project would never have incorporated gender, sexual orientation, gender identity, or disability. Allowing a group to be recognized only if it made an arbitrary historical cutoff (like 1964, when Congress passed the Civil Rights Act) would have been unjust. And closing the door now would be equally unfair. We didn't stand at the end of history then. We don't do so today.

It's also strange to insist that caring about some groups means not caring about others. Equality advocates often stand against a zero-sum mentality, insisting to opponents that compassion isn't a finite resource and that an inclusive society is better for everyone. We should work hard not to adopt the same cramped reasoning on our own side. Indeed, incorporating more groups into the conversation is usually an enhancement, not a dilution. We believe including considerations of gender and sexual orientation would offer a more nuanced understanding of a Black lesbian's experience than focusing on race alone. Similarly, we believe a Latino disabled veteran could feel more seen, not less, by a field that recognized veteran status as an important component of the project.

Even if you're unpersuaded by the conceptual case for welcoming new groups, you may find the strategic one compelling. When you dismiss new groups that tell you they're in pain, they don't slink away. They feel bitter, fueling the flames of backlash. Young men who are struggling in school, feeling adrift in a changing culture, or lacking meaningful work opportunities won't simply move on if supporters of the equality project tell them we only care about women. Rather, they'll seek support from the populist right, which is all too willing to channel male grievances into a toxic identity politics based on reasserting dominance over women. Many young men are already drawn to figures like social media personality Andrew Tate, who has called himself a misogynist and said women who put themselves "in a position to be raped" must "bear some responsibility" for that outcome. A Richard Reeves agenda is better than an Andrew Tate agenda.

Finally, we believe most people are capable of walking and chewing gum. In our presentations, we sometimes cite data showing 45 percent of straight white men feel pressure to minimize or downplay stigmatized aspects of their identity in the workplace, such as a mental or physical disability, religion, or socioeconomic status. The same data also show 83 percent of LGBTQ+ individuals and 79 percent of Black individuals experience the same pressure. Most people are perfectly able to absorb two insights from this data. Yes, straight white men should be included in the project of equality, as they have baskets of advantage and disadvantage like everyone else. And also: some groups experience more disadvantages than others—there's a big difference between 45 percent and 83 percent. In fact, we generally find straight white men are *more* willing to have the conversation about the unique barriers faced by LGBTQ+ individuals and Black individuals if their own struggles have been noticed and validated.

THE NEED TO MUDDLE THROUGH

Even with a posture of openness to new claims, the project of equality can't possibly encompass every social group. Some line-drawing is inevitable. One leader told us that although he was generally open to the claims of new cohorts, there would "never be a pickleball affinity group" at his organization.

So what's the difference between groups that should clearly be included in the project of equality (such as Jewish and Muslim individuals), those that clearly shouldn't (such as pickleball players), and those in the messy middle? The ultimate benchmark is whether the group currently experiences material or dignitary barriers that the project of equality could feasibly address. And the answer to this question can change over time. In the early 1900s when left-handed people were considered "primitive" and forced to write with their right hands, it would have made sense (had the field of DEI existed at the time) for the work to incorporate left-handedness. Now, not so much.

We realize this benchmark is imprecise. It asks us all to "muddle through" as we consider new claims together, rather than offering an algorithm for including or excluding certain groups. But the "muddling through" option is the only sensible way to proceed.

Our view is shaped by watching the Supreme Court wrestle with exactly this question. In the 1970s and '80s, the court tried to develop a formula to discern which groups were so disadvantaged in society that they should get enhanced protection from the courts (known as "heightened scrutiny"). The court started by setting out criteria: whether the group had suffered a history of discrimination, whether it was politically powerless, and whether it was marked by an immutable characteristic. This approach led to withering critiques. Weren't there other signs of social vulnerability the court should consider, like whether a group was relatively poor, experienced violence, or lacked access to healthcare (to suggest but a few)? And what did it mean to be politically powerless? Were women politically powerful because they were a majority of the population, or politically powerless because they held so few positions of authority in society? It turned out that group relations were far too complex to reduce to an equation.

In response to that complexity, the court attempted to shut down the entire project of giving groups heightened scrutiny. In a 1985 case, it refused to grant people with intellectual disabilities heightened scrutiny, noting that to do so could open the floodgates to other group claims, such as from "the aging, the disabled, the mentally ill, and the infirm." But the "shut it down" approach didn't work either. Even in the 1985 case, the court ended up ruling in favor of the plaintiffs with disabilities. And both before and after 1985, the court has chosen to protect many other groups it deemed unusually vulnerable without using a formula, including single people, gay people, and even "hippies." In short, it muddled through.

We understand the impulse to reach for a scientific answer for which groups are "in" or "out" of the project of equality. The Supreme Court's experience teaches us to resist that urge. Answering this question will be a matter of analysis, and also of politics and of intuition. But we'd like to set the field's default in the direction of openness to new claims. To maintain relevance in a constantly changing society, the project of equality must be one in which all Americans can see themselves.

STRATEGY 3 TAKEAWAYS

- The field of DEI has traditionally prioritized certain core classifications protected by anti-discrimination law, such as race and sex. This approach has stoked resentment among the groups that miss out. Supporters of the equality project should instead respond as a superhero would and go where the pain is.

- The project of equality should consider three kinds of claims by new groups seeking entry into the field: "claims of enforcement" (such as religion), "claims of symmetry" (such as boys and men), and "claims of extension" (such as class).

- The law is also pushing the project of equality to welcome new groups by making it harder to engage in race- and sex-based affirmative action.

- The project of equality can't possibly include every social group, and will inevitably draw lines. Deciding who's in and who's out will be a complex process of muddling through. But the default should be openness toward new claims rather than a reflexive opposition to them.

Strategy 4:
LEVEL THE PLAYING FIELD

Our spouses think we spend most of our time at work swanning from conference to conference at five-star resorts, where we schmooze for about an hour and then spend the rest of our time gadding about the glamorous city in which the conference is set. We keep insisting to them, truthfully, that a lot of events occur on tight budgets where we're stuck in an airless hotel conference room and nearly experience death by PowerPoint. One summit we attended, however, was almost a parody of the opulent confabs our spouses envision. It was in a sprawling resort with constantly circulating canapés served beside manicured pools with celebrity sightings galore.

In our defense, we were there to fight the good fight. The conference was a bipartisan one, and we'd been asked to debate an anti-DEI activist who believed all DEI was illegal. This belief has come to be a meme on the right. In 2024, Elon Musk—the businessman, former special advisor to the president, and apparently self-taught expert on the law—declared: "DEI is actually illegal, because it discriminates on the basis of race, sex, sexual preference, and all sorts of other things." In 2025, White House Deputy Chief of Staff Stephen Miller posted on social media that "DEI is illegal race-based discrimination in violation of the federal Civil Rights Act," echoing an earlier proclamation by his legal advocacy organization that "all DEI programs . . . based on race, national origin, or sex are illegal." The federal agency that enforces employment discrimination laws has even tried to make this assertion self-fulfilling by requiring some organizations with lawful DEI programs to use a label other than "DEI" to describe those programs.

There's just one problem with the pronouncement that all DEI is illegal: it's rubbish. Most DEI practices are absolutely legal. Some, like religious and disability accommodations, are even legally required. Nonetheless, the rabidly anti-DEI activist at the conference apparently believed this myth. And we really do mean "rabidly"—this was the kind of guy who danced on the graves of civil rights leaders with hobnailed boots. We also noticed that in seeking ideological balance, the conference organizers had seemingly overcorrected. The audience firmly leaned right.

We were in a lather in the green room trying to figure out how to proceed. The theme of the conference was to find "common ground" in our polarized nation. But what common ground could we possibly hold with someone who thought diversity initiatives were the work of the devil?

When the curtain rose, we said to him: "We know you think all DEI is illegal. So help us with this case study: in 1970, only five percent of top symphony orchestras were women. By 2016, that number had jumped to more than thirty-five percent. The fix was that they forced everyone to audition behind a screen so the directors couldn't see the gender of the musicians. So, tell us: is that strategy illegal?"

Our debate opponent almost scoffed and said: "Of course that practice is legal! It's the literal definition of gender-blindness to hide someone's gender so they can be evaluated on merit." The audience murmured assent.

We pounced: "We think you need to make a choice. Either you can say all DEI is illegal, or you can say the orchestra screen is legal. But you can't say both, because the orchestra screen is a DEI initiative." To his credit, he conceded the point. Confetti cannons exploded in the room. Or maybe that part was in our heads.

FROM LIFTING TO LEVELING

We tell this story to highlight two major categories of equality work: "lifting" and "leveling." A lifting strategy says: "This group of people has suffered historic and continuing disadvantage. Let's 'lift' them up with a preference." Had the symphony orchestras adopted the lifting strategy, they would have given women a "bump" in their audition score just because they were women. This strategy would have been like affirmative action programs in college admissions, where race was considered as a "plus factor."

Opponents like to frame the whole project of equality as a lifting enterprise. Ryan Williams, president of the Claremont Institute, argues: "The words that the acronym 'DEI' represent sound nice, but it is nothing more than affirmative action and racial preferences by a different name." Heather Mac Donald of the Manhattan Institute has also said that "diversity is simply a code word for preferences."

Yet there's another major type of equality work, which we call "leveling." A leveling strategy says: "Let's not give any group-specific bumps. Instead, let's use an identity-neutral approach to level the playing field." This strategy is what the orchestras actually embraced. Some orchestras even asked musicians to remove their shoes so the directors couldn't hear the clack of high heels on a hardwood floor. Researchers argue this simple fix increased a woman's chance of advancing through the audition process by 50 percent. Put differently, the orchestras recognized the status quo was biased in favor of men. In putting up the screens, they filtered out that bias.

Before the Supreme Court's 2023 affirmative action decision, organizations used both lifting and leveling strategies. After that decision, many lifting strategies are riskier, but leveling strategies are not. This is because lifting approaches, with every good intention, put a "thumb on the scale" for disadvantaged groups. The Supreme Court's "colorblind" philosophy makes such preferences hazardous. Leveling approaches, on the other hand, just make sure the scale is giving a true reading. They're legally unimpeachable, because they don't treat any groups differently from others. For that reason, the project of equality will have to rely more heavily on leveling practices going forward.

To be clear, our main objection to lifting practices is legal, not conceptual. In principle, lifting is often justified. Strategies like affirmative action promote integration and offset advantages held by dominant groups. But we also need to face legal reality and work with the strategies available. Fortunately, such strategies abound.

LEVELING STRATEGY #1: ANONYMIZE ASSESSMENTS

We love trotting out the orchestra screen example to confound and dismay our opponents. But not everyone is a fan. A dear colleague, who's been a champion of equality for decades, once asked us for the best defense of our work. Before we opened our mouths, he said: "And don't you dare talk about the orchestra screen. If you do, I'll straight-up murder you."

Edging away slightly, we asked why this example warranted such bile. "I'm not running a goddamn orchestra," he observed. "If I want to create an inclusive environment as a teacher, I have to know who my students are. I can't put up a screen between myself and the student I'm supervising. So even if the orchestra screen works, it's limited to that industry."

We disagree. All professors at NYU Law, including our colleague, grade our exams anonymously, meaning we don't know who wrote an exam until we submit the grade for it. It's a time-honored practice that protects our students and ourselves from our biases. Some teachers go further, routinely grading papers using anonymous identifiers like student IDs. In the workplace, hiring managers can use technology to strip out irrelevant demographic information from resumes, like the applicant's name or gender or undergraduate institution. They can also ask candidates to complete job-relevant skills tests and review the results with an assigned number or code, rather than linking the results to an individual's name. Judges for awards can review submissions of work (like essays or poems or films) without knowing who produced it. In Europe, where it's still common for job applicants to submit resumes with a photograph of themselves, employers can simply end that practice.

We think our colleague missed that the orchestra screen stands for a broader principle: if you can't discriminate *between* two people, you can't discriminate *against* one of them. For this reason, removing identity characteristics from important decisions can be a potent engine of fairness. Anonymous grading is a form of "colorblindness" and "gender-blindness" because it literally takes a person's race or gender out of consideration.

This colorblindness isn't the same as the "colorblindness" endorsed by the Supreme Court or by opponents of DEI. There's a world of difference between literal colorblindness and figurative colorblindness. If we're medically colorblind, we can't tell the difference between two colors, like red and green. But if we're legally or socially colorblind, we're not suggesting we can't tell the difference between, say, an Asian person and a white person. We mean that we *can* tell the difference, but we try to repress that knowledge. Often, that project of repression is impossible to the point of absurdity, as comedian Stephen Colbert has noted: "I don't see color. People tell me I'm white and I believe them, because police officers call me 'sir.'" Or: "I don't see race. People tell me I'm white and I believe them, because I own a lot of Jimmy Buffett albums." Even critics of DEI consider the metaphor misleading. As Coleman Hughes says, social "colorblindness" is like "warmheartedness"—it doesn't carry its literal meaning.

Where figurative colorblindness fails, however, literal colorblindness succeeds. If we know which student wrote which exam, we can try to repress that knowledge during the grading process and hope our good intentions override our biases. But if we're grading exams anonymously, we can be confident the student's race—or, for that matter, their gender, ethnicity, religion, nationality, or other characteristics—aren't influencing our judgment.

LEVELING STRATEGY #2: ADOPT STRUCTURED DECISION-MAKING

What was your last job interview like? If our experience is any guide, it was probably an unstructured "get to know you" conversation. Many organizations conduct open-ended interviews where the hiring manager asks whatever questions come to mind and assesses the candidate based on a "gut feel" for whether the person is a good "cultural fit." This method has been aptly described as involving a "stranded-in-the-airport" test. An investment banker described the test to sociologist Lauren Rivera: "Would I want to be stuck in an airport in Minneapolis in a snowstorm with them?"

Rivera deems unstructured interviews to be a breeding ground for bias, because "fit" is judged largely based on whether a candidate is similar to the interviewer. (This tendency is variously known as "similarity bias," "affinity bias," or "like likes like" bias.) Rivera's study of entry-level hiring practices at elite firms found that such assessments advantaged "job candidates who displayed affluent, white, and stereotypically masculine leisure pursuits and lifestyle markers."

To overcome affinity bias, organizations don't necessarily need to give a bump to less affluent, non-white, or stereotypically feminine candidates. Rather, it makes a tremendous difference just to level the playing field with a structured process: set job-related criteria for assessing candidates, ask interviewees the same questions, and score them against a formal rubric. Such a system reliably reduces bias, because it forces decision-makers to focus on what really matters for job performance. This solution applies to more than just job interviews. Feedback, performance evaluations, and promotion processes can also be structured, ensuring that candidates are measured against relevant criteria rather than whether their supervisor wants to hang out with them during a blizzard.

We saw the benefits of structured decision-making when we interviewed finalists for a leadership position at our university. Because this was an administrative role rather than a professorship, most applicants came from outside academia. We wanted to make sure the candidates had kept up with the latest research. So one of our standard questions was: "What piece of research in this field published in the last three years has been most influential?"

Shortly before the interviews began, we learned one of the finalists was a tenured professor. This created a mild dilemma. On the one hand, we'd committed to asking the same questions of all candidates. On the other, we feared it might come across as condescending to ask this question of an academic, who'd presumably be up to their eyeballs in the research. We resolved the dilemma in favor of structured interviewing, and asked the question of the professor as we did of the other candidates. To our surprise, the professor flubbed the question. He first mentioned a book that had been published more than a decade earlier, and when reminded of the three-year restriction, said he'd need to "think about it."

His non-answer was a significant mark against his candidacy and a revelation about our own (in this case, positive) biases. Had we not relied on structured interviewing, we would have imported our unfounded assumptions into the process.

LEVELING STRATEGY #3: AUDIT SYSTEMS FOR BIAS

Shelley Correll is a sociologist who has devoted her career to eliminating barriers for women. In a marquee project, she and her team combed through hundreds of performance reviews. She found that women were constantly being rated on their performance, while men were being rated on their potential. These ratings had a direct and negative effect on how quickly women could advance relative to men. Correll also offered prescriptions for organizations on how to eliminate this difference, like using formalized procedures and transparent assessment criteria.

When she spoke to us about this project, she'd just read an article we'd written on shifting from lifting work to leveling work. "I was really heartened by that piece," she said, "because the work we do has always been about de-biasing evaluation processes." She added: "I've always felt that just hiring a woman into a position—what you call 'lifting' work—is actually the easier thing to do. What we do—the 'leveling' work—is backbreaking. But it makes a more enduring difference."

Bias audits are, of course, not limited to performance reviews. Consider the work of Joan Williams, a legal scholar who studies and implements methods to interrupt bias in the workplace. Williams encourages organizations to keep track of two types of assignments: "career-enhancing work," meaning high-profile assignments that help employees succeed, and "office housework," like arranging meetings, cleaning cups in the office kitchen, and other routine tasks. Under her system, managers track whether they've assigned each of their employees career-enhancing work over the past month. Williams's team worked with an energy company that discovered that one of its departments was assigning career-enhancing work to 51 percent of men but only 38 percent of women. When managers received training on how to ensure fair access to opportunities and implemented a "tasking tool" to monitor assignments, the department completely closed the gender gap.

This work, like Correll's performance review project, is laborious. Yet it provides a model for the equality project that can be applied in a wide variety of settings. We once asked a student researcher at our center to audit all public-facing events and panel discussions hosted by our law school over the previous academic year. He found that speakers at these events were disproportionately male (65 percent) and white (74 percent). We shared this finding with law school leaders to encourage de-biasing of event management systems. Other studies have examined whether teachers have higher expectations of students from certain racial or ethnic backgrounds (yes), and whether demographic disparities arise in the language used in recommendation letters (also yes). Organizations that do their own self-audits on topics like these could use such information to design better internal systems, or develop educational programs to nudge leaders toward less biased decision-making.

When auditing systems, sometimes you'll discover that even simple processes have surprising biases built into them. One study found that a teaching evaluation system that rated university faculty on a scale from one to ten disadvantaged women, whereas a simple adjustment from a ten-point scale to a six-point scale nearly erased the gender gap. Why? The researchers argue the top score on a ten-point scale evokes the idea of "perfect performance," and gender stereotypes relating to professional perfection mean that women are less likely to receive that score. A six-point scale, by contrast, allows for "a wider variety of performances" to receive top marks.

The researchers take this finding and urge organizations to study other components of the "architecture of evaluation," not just numerical rating scales. They note various factors that might also influence disparities in performance appraisals, such as the order or wording of question prompts, whether evaluations are anonymous, whether evaluations are completed by individuals or groups, and whether they're conducted online or offline. There's plenty of room for experimentation. Again, what's notable is that identifying and removing bias from systems doesn't give "preference" to anyone, and is entirely consistent with the law.

LEVELING STRATEGY #4: CREATE FORMAL MENTORSHIP PROGRAMS

A firm once engaged us to educate their leaders on how to address a mentorship gap. Like many organizations in corporate America, this firm had a disproportionately high number of white men in leadership positions. This meant leaders would often feel a natural connection with junior white men who reminded them of themselves. Some leaders would walk past younger male employees' offices on a Friday afternoon and casually invite them out for a beer. They'd throw footballs around in the hallways and open meetings with chitchat about local sports teams. They'd also go out golfing and hunting together on the weekends, often with clients. This bonding did more than cement social relationships; it also served as informal mentorship. Young white men who "fit the mold" would get special access to senior leaders and clients. Women and people of color wouldn't.

Sociologists Frank Dobbin and Alexandra Kalev recommend a solution: "create a formal program that offers a mentor to everyone." This approach to mentorship differs from those that rely on informal connections, which are subject to all the biases and inequalities this firm experienced. It also differs from programs that limit formal mentorship only to workers at particular levels or to those who have shown exceptional promise as "high potential" employees.

Even though a formal program of the kind recommended by Dobbin and Kalev is identity-neutral, it tends to benefit people of color and women the most. Their research has found that women of color are the largest beneficiaries of formal mentorship programs, as "they have the most trouble finding mentors when mentoring is informal." Once again, while a rising tide lifts all boats, it lifts the ones at a lower starting point more. And of course, mentorship programs don't only apply in corporate settings. Schools, universities, and any other large institutions can establish programs to match people to mentors and close gaps that prevent certain groups from getting the support they need to advance.

LEVELING STRATEGIES ARE POPULAR

While the shift from lifting to leveling could be justified on legal grounds alone, it also resonates deeply with the general public. A 2024 Manhattan Institute survey of 2,100 voters found that when respondents were asked which of two ideas they preferred for addressing racial inequality, only 21 percent agreed with a statement that sounded like lifting: "We should focus on creating a race-conscious society to repair the harms of the past by developing policies that benefit marginalized groups." In contrast, majorities across all demographic groups favored a statement that sounded more like leveling: "We should focus on creating a colorblind society where everyone is treated equally regardless of the color of their skin."

While the Manhattan Institute is a conservative think tank, this finding jibes with other polling. A 2024 national Bellwether Research survey of more than three thousand American voters found that a statement justifying diversity programs because they "correct past and existing injustices and unfair practices that hold people back" was the least effective of eight pro-DEI messages the research firm tested. We suspect this statement failed to resonate because lifting practices could appear to give people a boost for reasons other than their individual talents and achievements.

In contrast, the three most effective pro-diversity messages in the Bellwether survey emphasized leveling. They underscored how the values of diversity, equity, and inclusion allow "everyone to reach their full potential," help "make sure the door is open wide enough so that people who have traditionally had less access to opportunities get the chance to be considered," and "reflect our shared vision for a country where everyone, regardless of background, has a fair shot at success." These messages are all about expanding equal opportunity, but don't mention bumps or preferences.

In our work with organizations, we're often asked for pithy formulations of what language to avoid and what language to embrace. "I've never been one to stay quiet about inclusion," one leader told us, "but I'm so terrified of getting sued that I'm biting my tongue these days. Can you give me a quick 'from this, to that' example?" We offered him, and many others, the following formulations. Move away from statements like this: "Organizations should lift up historically marginalized groups to compensate for the disadvantage they have suffered." Move toward statements like this: "Talent is everywhere but opportunity is not, and equality work closes the gap."

The unpopularity of lifting and popularity of leveling helps explain why most Americans supported the Supreme Court's decision to end affirmative action in higher education, and why even liberal California couldn't get voters to restore affirmative action in that state when the issue went up for a vote in 2020. Popularity isn't everything, and we count ourselves among the minority who continue to support affirmative action in principle. But enabling the work of equality to succeed requires addressing not just legal constraints, but also political and social ones. Moving from lifting to leveling does just that.

LEVELING STRATEGIES MAKE THE WORK NARROWER BUT CAN ALSO MAKE IT DEEPER

The legal restrictions on lifting practices have certainly narrowed the project of equality, but they may, counterintuitively, also deepen it.

To begin with the narrowing point, let's acknowledge that taking lifting strategies off the board is a loss. While leveling strategies are legally safe and socially popular, they're not a panacea. They level the playing field when the players are competing, but do nothing to address the inequalities that happened before the game. This shortcoming is why lifting practices emerged in the first place: they help people "ramp up" to a level playing field.

Take college admissions. Let's say you don't attend a top-tier high school, don't have access to tutors and test prep services, or don't have the resources necessary to cultivate a rich set of extracurricular activities. A "leveling" admissions process will probably assess you as an inferior candidate compared with applicants from more advantaged economic backgrounds. This is a playing field on which many bright students never even have the opportunity to compete.

The orchestra screen initiative illustrates this point. While it has succeeded in raising the number of women in symphony orchestras, the screen hasn't improved racial and ethnic diversity. Anthony Tommasini, a classical music critic, makes the case starkly: "If the musicians onstage are going to better reflect the diversity of the communities they serve, the audition process has to be altered to take into fuller account artists' backgrounds and experiences. Removing the screen is a crucial step."

The shift away from lifting practices undoubtedly removes tools from the equality project's toolbox. But supporters of equality need not despair. By embracing leveling practices, advocates have an opportunity to make the work of equality significantly deeper than it was previously.

Before the legal and social backlash, some organizations adopted "broad but shallow" equality work—hosting slapdash DEI training sessions without assessing their rigor, appointing people to diversity positions without giving them adequate budget or influence to be successful, running a set of scattershot programs built around heritage months like Hispanic Heritage Month and Native American History Month, and focusing on recruitment with little attention to whether newly diverse hires were treated fairly after they arrived. This approach has led to a widespread perception that DEI is ineffective. In a 2025 *Axios* poll, a majority of Americans said DEI had neither benefited nor hindered their career, but rather had made "no impact" whatsoever. A plurality of respondents in a separate 2025 poll similarly reported that DEI makes no difference in addressing discrimination. These are the studies that make our hair turn gray (or grayer). Now organizations have an opportunity to double down on "narrow but deep" equality work, which might ultimately be more effective and lead to a change in public perception.

What do we mean by "deep" work? We mean work that pulls apart the architecture of organizational decisions, then rebuilds those systems to create equal opportunity. We've already offered several examples, such as anonymized assessments, structured interviewing, bias audits, and mentorship programs. But this list is only the beginning. Dobbin and Kalev offer other research-backed ideas. Workplaces can make shift schedules for hourly workers more consistent, and also allow such workers to swap shifts. That combination of predictability and flexibility has been shown to support retention and advancement of people of color and women. They can also use formal "referral programs" to encourage employees to refer friends and family members for jobs, which boosts diversity more than traditional recruitment efforts. The diversity implications of these initiatives aren't necessarily intuitive, which means organizations can test different interventions to see what works.

Even Andrea Lucas, the Trump-appointed head of the Equal Employment Opportunity Commission, endorses a wide array of "deep" practices that avoid race- and sex-based preferences while nonetheless advancing the goal of equality. It's worth sharing several of Lucas's recommendations to show how much equality work is still available even in our constrained legal and political environment:

- Audit job descriptions to remove unnecessary prerequisites, such as degree requirements.
- Post promotion opportunities and automatically consider all candidates at a certain level, rather than waiting for eligible employees to raise their hands.
- Implement standardized leadership development training for all employees at a particular level.
- Adopt training programs, employee resource groups, mentorship programs, and internship programs specifically for "first-generation" professionals to help advance social mobility.
- Expand the pool of applicants by recruiting from a wider range of colleges (for jobs requiring a college degree) and by advertising jobs in a variety of formats that reach different audiences (including in multiple languages).

- Rethink the culture of overwork in leadership and executive roles, because that culture has a disproportionate negative impact on women who are caregivers, first-generation professionals, immigrant employees, and employees from less advantaged economic backgrounds.

Again, all of these recommendations come from a virulent *opponent* of DEI.

"Deep" work, then, involves taking apart and reconstructing a wide variety of organizational systems, including outreach, resume screening, student admissions, interviewing, onboarding, work assignments, discipline, award conferrals, standardized testing, mentorship, performance evaluations and expectations, promotion, job referrals, feedback, layoffs, and how meetings and classroom conversations are conducted. This work is "narrow" in the sense that it avoids affirmative action or other race- or sex-based bumps. But it's "deep" because it digs into every institutional nook and cranny to ensure fairness across the board. It's leveling on steroids.

To go back to the orchestra example, one possible reason the screen doesn't improve racial and ethnic diversity in orchestras is that it's administered only at the time of the audition, not in all the years leading up to that moment. For instance, the screen does nothing to redress racial disparities in access to instruments, lessons, musical summer programs, conservatories, or other opportunities along the path to the audition process. But what if leveling strategies were applied at every point in that longer stream of time, and not just at the audition? This would mean leveling in music programs from preschool to performing arts school, with leaders at each phase working hard to ensure people of all racial and ethnic backgrounds have the same opportunities, feedback, and resources to express their talents.

Opponents of DEI may gripe that such deep work would involve a vast project of social engineering. If they do, we can quote them back to themselves. Andrea Lucas says she wants "equal employment opportunity." The Trump administration's foremost anti-DEI executive order calls for "restoring merit-based opportunity." And let's not forget the Supreme Court, which said in its *Students for Fair Admissions* decision that "eliminating racial discrimination means eliminating all of it." Opponents of DEI have tied themselves to these principles.

Now supporters of equality have an opportunity to define what such principles mean in practice. If we do so effectively, opponents may come to regret endorsing nondiscrimination and equal opportunity so energetically. A project of eliminating *all* discrimination would require a movement more sweeping than anything the nation has ever seen.

STRATEGY 4 TAKEAWAYS

- Two major categories of equality work are "lifting" strategies (which confer preferences on disadvantaged groups) and "leveling" strategies (which use identity-neutral practices to level the playing field for all).

- In the new legal landscape, lifting practices can be legally risky, while leveling practices are perfectly safe. Leveling strategies are also more popular with the American public.

- Leveling strategies include anonymizing assessments, using structured decision-making, auditing systems for bias, and creating formal mentorship programs.

- Moving from lifting to leveling makes the project of equality narrower, but it could also make it deeper. Organizations can dig into every aspect of their processes (such as interviewing, mentorship, feedback, and promotion systems) to identify bias, then rebuild those systems to create equal opportunity across the board.

Strategy 5:
EMBRACE THE UNIVERSAL

Barely a month after the Supreme Court gutted affirmative action, Edward Blum—the anti-DEI architect of that litigation—filed another lawsuit that sent shockwaves through the DEI community. On this occasion, his target wasn't an elite university, but an Atlanta-based venture capital firm called the Fearless Fund.

At the time, the Fearless Fund operated a program called the "Strivers Grant Contest," which awarded $20,000 grants to small businesses owned by Black women. The contest aimed to close a shocking disparity—less than half a percent of venture capital funding went to Black women entrepreneurs. Blum argued the program was "unjust and polarizing." His organization claimed the contest violated a federal civil rights law from 1866 prohibiting race discrimination in the formation or enforcement of contracts. This law was enacted after the Civil War to ensure formerly enslaved people could fully participate in the American economy. Now Blum was wielding that law against the Black community.

Blum didn't stop there. On the heels of the Fearless Fund lawsuit, his organization filed suits against three major law firms. Each firm offered a diversity fellowship program that was only open to law students from groups underrepresented in the legal profession. Blum's lawsuits argued the programs discriminated on the basis of race. As the months went by, the number of lawsuits against similar programs swelled. McDonald's was sued for a scholarship program it offered to high schoolers with "at least one parent of Hispanic/Latino heritage." Hidden Star, a nonprofit organization that helps disadvantaged entrepreneurs, was sued for a "Galaxy Grant" contest that limited eligibility to "minority and women entrepreneurs." The National Museum of the American Latino was sued for its internship program for Latino students.

In the first couple years after the Supreme Court's *Students for Fair Admissions* decision, dozens of lawsuits like these were filed against what we call "targeted programs"—initiatives such as scholarships, grants, internships, and fellowships specifically reserved for underrepresented groups. Lawsuits challenging targeted programs quickly became the largest category of anti-DEI lawsuits we were tracking. Nearly all such lawsuits invoked the 1866 civil rights law and the Supreme Court's decision. They contended that targeted programs were illegal for not allowing certain groups (like white men) to apply. And while lots of these cases are still working their way through the courts, the legal risk is real. We can't imagine today's conservative supermajority Supreme Court allowing many programs to categorically exclude white individuals or men. The Fearless Fund seems to agree: after losing in a lower court, it closed its grant program rather than appeal to the Supreme Court.

These developments are a body blow to the project of equality. Targeted programs exist because of a need that a particular community faces, like gaps in funding or representation. Organizations then adopt a remedy to address that specific need. Before the Supreme Court's decision, many organizations had developed scholarships or internships restricted to students of color, mentorship programs and leadership retreats restricted to women, or affinity groups restricted to LGBTQ+ people. Since then, as they've watched the tsunami of lawsuits, many of those organizations have opened their programs to everyone. This shift from targeted participation to universal participation threatens to dilute or destroy the whole purpose of the programs. Yet while we regret having to make these adjustments, we believe much good work can be done through universalist strategies.

THE PROMISE AND PITFALLS OF UNIVERSALISM

Universalism has always been a core part of our own approach to equality. We believe the end goal of equality efforts should be a society in which everybody, including people from dominant or majority groups, feels a sense of belonging. We also strive for a society in which group identities like race or gender are mostly less, not more, salient in our interactions with one another. Our research center's website reflected this philosophy long before the Supreme Court's decision by proudly stating that "we strive for the universal" and believe "a culture of inclusion is better for everyone."

Some progressives deride our approach. We once had a student describe our center's mission to us as "vague," "toothless," and aimed at benefiting "a white, straight majority" instead of marginalized people. Ouch. We disagree with this student's assessment and are unapologetic about our emphasis on universalism. But it's important to distinguish our approach from another universalist approach this student may have had in mind.

When people urge universalism, what they sometimes mean is that we should ignore group-based inequalities. Like toddlers playing "hide and seek" who think they can make themselves disappear by putting their hands in front of their face, this form of universalism thinks we can make group-based conflicts and injustices go away merely by pretending they don't exist. Exhibit A for this phenomenon is the "All Lives Matter" meme. In response to the ubiquitous "Black Lives Matter" slogan after the murder of George Floyd in 2020, a counter-meme developed that said "All Lives Matter." It was an appealing rejoinder for many, because all lives obviously *do* matter. But as one wag pointed out, saying "All Lives Matter" at that moment was like going to a stranger's funeral and yelling, "I too have felt loss!" In practice, the slogan came across as "Please stop talking about the challenges faced by the Black community." In moving too abruptly to the universal, it ran away from the conversation Black Lives Matter was trying to start.

An earlier catastrophic example of failed universalism is the military's "don't ask, don't tell" policy. This 1993 policy was meant to be an advance over the previous one, which stated that "homosexuality is incompatible with military service." But as the moniker suggests, under "don't ask, don't tell," both the military leadership and gay service members were all supposed to pretend that gay people didn't serve in the military. This was done in the name of unity: the justification was that the known presence of a gay person would destroy "unit cohesion" within a platoon. Yet by insisting that no one was to speak about gay people's existence, the policy was a bit like asking people not to think about pink elephants. Gay people were at least as visible in the military as they were before, and more than thirteen thousand service members were discharged for homosexuality under the new policy.

We call the All Lives Matter or "don't ask, don't tell" approaches "unearned universalism," because they demand an immediate shift from a group register to a universal register without requiring anyone to see or fix group-based injustices. This shift might save dominant groups from uncomfortable conversations or even preserve a surface-level peace, but it ultimately fosters more division because it leaves marginalized groups feeling (correctly) that their issues have been ignored.

Instead, we favor "earned universalism." This approach agrees with the goals of unifying and generally reducing the salience of group identity. But it believes we all must *earn* the pivot to the universal by showing we care about, and seek to address, group disparities and biases on the path to achieving those goals. Let's say you're a leader at a predominantly white university trying to make the institution more inclusive for students of color. If you're an unearned universalist, you'd say: "Let's not talk about race and focus instead on our common humanity." If you're an earned universalist, you'd say: "Let's talk about race so we can identify any barriers students of color face in our institution. Then let's remove those barriers so we can all come together."

Many opponents of the equality project favor unearned universalism— they want organizations to shut down their targeted programs without doing anything to solve the inequalities that caused those programs to exist. But organizations can embrace the universalism that the law increasingly demands in an earned, rather than unearned, way. One method of doing so is by shifting from "cohorts to content." Another is by shifting from "cohorts to character."

THE SHIFT FROM COHORTS TO CONTENT

Many years ago, we launched a course for law students called "Leadership, Diversity, and Inclusion," which combined equality theory with skills training on topics like negotiation, written communication, and oral presentations. We developed the course to help students who'd previously lacked equal opportunity to develop these professional skills. Yet we deliberately opened it to "all students with an interest in diversity and inclusion (broadly defined)." We've offered the course regularly since then.

The supermajority of students who've signed up for the course belong to one marginalized group or another. However, some students from more conventionally advantaged backgrounds have used the course to learn about the barriers faced by their peers, or to make the case for expanding the field of DEI to encompass additional concerns, like religion or mental health. Such students have contributed enormously to the class, and many of them have continued to advance the values of inclusion in their workplaces after graduation.

After the *Students for Fair Admissions* decision, some anxious students asked if we'd have to scuttle this course, given all the attacks on DEI. Our answer was an emphatic "no." While the law prohibits programs from excluding people based on characteristics like race, it still allows programs to be thematized around those topics. As we put it, the distinction is between "cohort"-based restrictions (which are legally risky if they concern classifications like race or sex) and "content"-based restrictions (which are legally permissible).

This distinction between cohorts and content may seem subtle, but it has momentous consequences. Consider the contrast between two of President Trump's executive orders. The first executive order, issued in January 2025, accused major institutions of using "dangerous, demeaning, and immoral race- and sex-based preferences under the guise of so-called 'diversity, equity, and inclusion.'" It then tasked the executive branch of the federal government with rooting out such "illegal, pernicious discrimination."

Barely three months later, the same administration issued an executive order that purported to promote "Excellence and Innovation at Historically Black Colleges and Universities" (HBCUs). HBCUs are educational institutions founded prior to the Civil Rights Act of 1964 to offer Black students higher education at a time when most colleges excluded them. The order praised HBCUs as "integral to American students' pursuit of prosperity and wellbeing, providing the pathway to a career and a better life," and described them as "beacons of educational excellence and economic opportunity."

So even as one executive order attacked DEI, another lauded HBCUs. What explains this discrepancy? The most principled way of reconciling these two executive orders is that, in the eyes of the administration, DEI programs use cohort-based restrictions by giving preference to people based on race or sex. HBCUs, on the other hand, are content-based. While their missions often emphasize values like diversity, or highlight expertise in scholarship affecting the Black community, they allow anyone to apply, regardless of their race.

This distinction between cohorts and content means organizations can save cohort-based initiatives by redesigning them as content-based programs. The strategy has already proven to be an amulet against legal liability. The three law firms sued by Blum had diversity fellowships that restricted who could apply to them on demographic grounds. One of the firms, Morrison Foerster, had a fellowship only open to "a diverse population that has historically been underrepresented in the legal profession." Instead of shutting down its program like the Fearless Fund, the firm opened its fellowship to all applicants, regardless of their demographic background. It nevertheless required applicants to have "a demonstrated commitment to diversity and inclusion in the legal profession." After the firm made this change from cohorts to content, Blum dropped his lawsuit. He did the same with the two other firms when they made similar changes.

This strategy has been a winner in other industries as well. McDonald's settled the lawsuit against its scholarship program for Hispanic or Latino high schoolers by opening the scholarship to "any student who can demonstrate an impact on or commitment to the Latino community." The University of Colorado School of Medicine, which previously offered a scholarship for "groups recognized as historically underrepresented in medicine," opened the program to "all applicants" with a focus "on those who have had personal experience overcoming hardship or have an interest in working with or advocating for patients who have traditionally experienced barriers to accessing health care." It too settled a lawsuit by making this shift. The content of these programs remained focused on advancing the interests of a particular community or upholding a set of equality-related values. But people of any cohort could apply and participate.

THE SHIFT FROM COHORTS TO CHARACTER

Before the Supreme Court renders a decision, it typically holds an "oral argument" where the parties get to make their case before the court, and the justices get to pepper them with questions. Usually these oral arguments are dry, technical affairs that would put anyone who's not a lawyer or journalist into a coma. Occasionally, however, one of the justices seizes the public's attention with a mic-drop moment. This is what happened during the oral argument in the *Students for Fair Admissions* case. Justice Ketanji Brown Jackson, who'd only joined the court four months earlier, raised a trenchant hypothetical scenario that revealed the unfairness of a blanket "colorblind" rule in college admissions.

Justice Jackson asked the lawyer seeking to end affirmative action to imagine two applicants to the University of North Carolina. The first applicant says his family has lived in the North Carolina area since before the Civil War, and that he wants to attend the university to honor his family's legacy and become the fifth generation to graduate from that institution. The second applicant also says his family has lived in the North Carolina area since before the Civil War, but observes that "they were slaves and never had a chance to attend this venerable institution." He notes that as an African American student, he now has the opportunity to honor his family's legacy by attending the university.

Justice Jackson noted that a prohibition on race-conscious admissions would allow the first applicant to tell his story, but might prevent the second applicant from telling his, because the second applicant's story is "bound up with his race and with the race of his ancestors." She observed that such an outcome might itself violate the Constitution's Equal Protection Clause.

When the Supreme Court released its decision, Justice Jackson was in dissent. The court did, in fact, adopt the blanket colorblind rule she'd critiqued. But we think Justice Jackson's influence is visible in a loophole the court's majority left open at the end of the opinion. After dismantling affirmative action, the opinion stated that universities could still consider "an applicant's discussion of how race affected his or her life, be it through discrimination, inspiration, or otherwise." In other words, schools couldn't give any racial group an automatic bump in the admissions process. But if an individual wrote about their race in the application essay, the university could choose students based on the content of that essay.

The difference between these two preferences, the court explained, was that the categorical bump made assumptions about the entire group, while the second bump for the essay didn't. The second bump, after all, reflects an applicant's personal characteristics like their courage, determination, or leadership abilities. "The student must be treated based on his or her experiences as an individual," the court stated, "not on the basis of race." In our language, the court sees a big difference between focusing on a person's "cohort" and focusing on their "character."

Some organizations have happily jumped through the court's loophole. The medical partnership Vituity previously offered a sign-on bonus for Black physicians. After it got sued for racial discrimination, it settled the suit by agreeing that when selecting recipients for bonuses, it would "only take into consideration how race affected a physician's life, be it through discrimination, inspiration, or otherwise." (Bonus points to Vituity for directly quoting the Supreme Court opinion!) The Small Business Administration, a federal government agency, has also used essays to determine which small business owners should receive government support on account of being "disadvantaged." In the educational realm, many selective colleges now ask applicants to discuss race or other aspects of their identity in personal statements.

Despite these examples, the practice of using an applicant's discussion of their identity to determine access to opportunities isn't yet widespread outside of educational settings. This is puzzling, because the shift from cohorts to character is a remarkably broad exception. Organizations could require essays to dock in the safe harbor the court has created. And the court's opinion isn't limited to essays. It also encompasses any "discussion" of race that bears on an individual's non-racial attributes. Organizations could ask candidates to talk about "how race has affected your life, be it through discrimination, inspiration, or otherwise" in interviews for jobs or promotions. They could use the same question as a prompt when selecting candidates for fellowships, mentorship programs, retreats, scholarships, grants, or any other opportunity. The applicant's discussion could be verbal or written, one paragraph long or a full-length narrative. The exception could also extend beyond race to gender, socioeconomic status, or any of the applicant's other social identities. And although the court's decision was made in relation to higher education, its logic carries into other areas like employment, contracting, and grantmaking.

DO PROGRAMS *REALLY* NEED TO BE UNIVERSAL?

We once got roped into an employee town hall meeting at a hospitality company by some nervous executives. These top leaders, including the company's head lawyer and the chief inclusion officer, were explaining recent changes the organization had made to its diversity policies.

The chief inclusion officer said that the company had previously allowed its affinity groups (such as the Black employees group, the women's group, and the LGBTQ+ group) to limit meetings only to people who belong to those demographics. She gave the examples of allowing the Black affinity group to meet with just Black members after the murder of George Floyd in 2020, and allowing the Asian and Pacific Islander affinity group to exclude non-Asians when discussing the spike in hate crimes against people of Asian ancestry during the COVID-19 pandemic. She then observed that the company had decided to open these groups to everyone: "The bottom line is that even if you don't belong to the relevant demographic group, you have the right to attend any affinity group meeting." Finally, she added a twist: "But understand that you're treading on sacred space and you should probably think twice about being there."

Immediately after the comment, we watched the company's head lawyer literally spring into action. She leaped in front of the chief inclusion officer and practically shouted: "Disregard that last sentence—that's not organization policy! Anyone can go to any meeting regardless of identity!" It was the closest we've come to seeing one corporate executive jump-tackle another.

What the lawyer knew that the chief inclusion officer (understandably) didn't was that the law requires compliance in reality, not just on the surface. As the Supreme Court has said, "what cannot be done directly cannot be done indirectly." Prior to the Civil War, the law denied voting rights to Black individuals. After the Civil War, the Fifteenth Amendment prohibited race discrimination in voting. But rather than fully extending the franchise as the Constitution demanded, lawmakers found more subtle ways to block voting rights. For instance, they used literacy tests as a requirement to vote, knowing this would disproportionately screen out Black voters, given their inability to access education at the time. It's now well established in civil rights law that you can't engage in these "pretextual" shenanigans.

The same logic applies to equality initiatives today. In its 2023 affirmative action decision, the court anticipated that universities might want to circumvent the ban on race-conscious admissions by using other strategies to engage in affirmative action by stealth. The ruling clearly prohibited such workarounds: "Universities may not simply establish through application essays or other means the regime we hold unlawful today."

For this reason, any legally required changes to diversity policies must be more than cosmetic. In one unfortunate example, an administrator at

Belmont University described the institution's Office of Hope, Unity, and Belonging (HUB) by noting: "The HUB is hope, unity, and belonging. That's DEI. Let's be real.... We're always going to keep doing what we're doing. The work never stops. We just change on how we talk about it.... We just changed the terminology and the language that we use." This statement led a U.S. representative to demand an investigation into the university. Whether or not the administrator's statement was accurate or a verbal slip, leaders would be well advised to avoid such rhetoric. When the law requires DEI to change, it must change in substance, not just form.

WHAT'S LOST

We've described two ways pro-equality organizations can make their programs universal while retaining a focus on diversity. One is to move from cohorts to content—allowing anyone to participate so long as they're committed to the content of the program. The other is to move from cohorts to character—allowing anyone to participate whose life experience connects to the program. In case we sound overly upbeat about these shifts, we want to enter an important caveat. Moving from targeted programs to universal programs comes with a number of costs.

A shift to the universal might make the program harder to administer. As we've noted, organizations can't legally exclude people based on race, but they can legally consider how an applicant's race has informed other non-racial attributes such as their resilience, determination, or leadership skills. Making this distinction is a tightrope walk. Some organizations might worry that in practice, the administrators reviewing the essays will slip into illegal decision-making by subtly favoring members of underrepresented racial groups.

It's also often inefficient or even impossible to assess each person's story one by one. When trying to decide which employees to invite to a diversity conference, it's much easier to limit attendance by inviting only the members of the various affinity groups for Black, Latino, Asian, LGBTQ+, and disabled employees than to ask everyone in the organization to write an essay describing how their identity has affected their life and then devote personnel to evaluate those essays. And when budgets are limited, it might not be feasible to invite everyone anyway.

Another downside of the shift to the universal is the toll it can place on program applicants. In particular, requiring people to write essays dredging up their experiences of bias can create significant burdens for the writers. After the Small Business Administration required disadvantaged business owners to write essays, some applicants hired lawyers to help them craft their narratives. One of those lawyers, Nicole Pottroff, noted that many applicants wrote about "sexual harassment," "blatant racism," and other topics "that were very hurtful to the individual telling the story." "Most of this is painful," Pottroff said, as the writers were "hoping to repress a lot of these memories." Even where essay writers don't disclose experiences of trauma, they may feel pressure to play up certain aspects of their identity to appeal to admissions officers or hiring managers. Legal scholar Justin Driver points out that prior to the *Students for Fair Admissions* decision, Black college applicants could check a racial box but then write personal statements about their passion for "Proust, Plato, string theory, 'The Odyssey,' or anything else under the university's vast sun." Now, as Driver notes, such students have an incentive to "produce narratives of racial woe." People might find it uncomfortable, at best, to force their life story into prefabricated templates that a decision-maker will find inspiring or heart-wrenching.

Perhaps the deepest cost of shifting to the universal is the impact on the communities that previously participated in targeted programs. We once advised Audrey, a head of human resources for a healthcare organization. She was considering what the organization should do about its annual retreat for employees of color. In the new legal environment, she had to decide whether to shut down the retreat altogether or open it to everyone. She decided to open it to everyone, but retain diversity as the theme of the retreat—a classic move from cohorts to content. From her perspective, she'd saved the retreat from being canceled. She'd also secured additional funding to cover the anticipated costs of more people attending. She sent out a cheerful announcement to this effect.

She thought she'd be hailed as a hero. Instead, she met hurricane-force blowback from the employees of color who had attended the retreat in prior years. Those employees told Audrey they understood the legal reasons behind her decision. However, they objected to the "toxic positivity" with which she rolled out the change. In their view, Audrey's chipper message suggested that she either didn't know, or was feigning ignorance about, why the retreat was important in the first place. As one employee explained, the whole reason people of color needed to "retreat" from the organization was because they often had a different experience from white employees. Having a space where they could speak frankly among others who shared their experience helped them overcome isolation and build resilience. Opening the retreat to all comers would flatly preclude at least some of those candid conversations.

We sympathized with Audrey because we thought the retreat should be opened to everyone. But we counseled her to clarify at the next opportunity that she didn't mean to paper over the real downside of doing so. (She took this tack and it went over well.) And now when we counsel other organizations that are making their programs universal, we encourage them to acknowledge what's been lost before moving on to the more positive aspects of this shift.

WHAT'S GAINED

While the downsides are real, we believe the shift to universalism helps the cause of equality in a number of ways.

Universal programs encourage effective allyship. An ally is someone who leverages their advantages in support of others who lack those same advantages, such as a man who cares about women's rights or a white individual who supports racial justice efforts. The project of equality relies heavily on allies, as they by definition have more power than marginalized groups. Yet well-meaning allies often hesitate to participate in equality initiatives due to a lack of "psychological standing," meaning they don't want to crash a party intended for others. This hesitation hurts the project of equality, because research shows allies are often better situated than marginalized groups to advocate for diversity and challenge bias. One study found that women and people of color received diminished performance and competence ratings when they pushed for hiring more members of underrepresented groups, while white men were spared this penalty. Other studies have found that members of dominant groups are taken more seriously than members of targeted groups when they confront non-inclusive behavior. Fairly or not, allies are probably viewed as less self-interested when they speak up for diversity. Opening programs to everybody could help allies increase their knowledge and develop their advocacy skills by giving them a clear invitation to enter the equality project.

A more subtle benefit of universal programs is the message sent to dominant group members who *don't* consider themselves to be allies. Usually, the focus of opening up targeted programs is to ensure the benefits will be available to all. It should also help ensure the responsibility to do this work is placed on everyone. Targeted programs give members of dominant groups an excuse to opt out of the project of equality, as they aren't eligible to participate in many initiatives anyway. This contributes to a perception that the project of equality is the responsibility of marginalized group members. In our work, we constantly hear complaints from students, colleagues, and employees from marginalized backgrounds that they are the ones burdened with the task of making their institutions more inclusive, while members of dominant groups get to carry on with their studies or their jobs. If you go to a town hall meeting on diversity, it's a good bet that someone will say: "The people who really need to hear this are not in the room." Embracing universality puts pressure on everyone in an organization to pitch in. Organizations can turn the work of equality from a niche responsibility performed by underrepresented groups into a contribution required of all.

A final important benefit of universal programs is that they trigger less resistance—not just legally, but socially. Targeted programs that exclude certain groups from accessing grants, scholarships, or employment opportunities can cause the people who miss out to feel bitter. Those individuals, rightly or not, often perceive the recipients as getting "special treatment." By including everybody, universal programs take this resentment off the table.

BEYOND THE ZERO-SUM GAME

We've mostly spoken about universalism in terms of program design—shifting from cohort-based restrictions to other eligibility criteria. But a shift to the universal isn't just about who gets to participate in an internship or a scholarship. It's much more about a different conception of the equality project itself. The traditional way of framing equality efforts is that they only help members of specific marginalized groups like people of color, women, people with disabilities, and LGBTQ+ individuals. A newer and now essential way of framing the project of equality is that it also helps everyone, even those who belong to dominant or majority groups.

Some situations are, of course, zero sum. When multiple individuals are competing over a limited number of college admission slots or job opportunities, some candidates will "win" and others will "lose." As the Supreme Court noted in its 2023 affirmative action decision: "College admissions are zero-sum. A benefit provided to some applicants but not to others necessarily advantages the former group at the expense of the latter." Opponents of the project of equality like to fixate on these situations to feed the narrative that DEI is unfair. We're troubled whenever the public conversation centers on zero-sum situations, because research shows that people who have a zero-sum mindset are less likely to support diversity and inclusion efforts in general.

Fortunately, a multitude of equality initiatives benefit all. Policy advocate Angela Glover Blackwell coined the term "curb-cut effect" to describe how policies designed to help some people can end up helping everyone. Blackwell notes that curb cuts created for wheelchair users also help people with strollers, luggage, or other heavy items, as well as skateboarders, runners, or anyone else who wants a smoother path on and off the sidewalk. Parental leave, initially established to support working mothers, is increasingly being taken by fathers as well, who view it as a vital opportunity to bond with their children. Captioning of meetings and video content, which was created to support hearing-impaired people, is now widely used by viewers without disabilities to aid comprehension. In fact, one study found that 80 percent of video caption users don't have a hearing impairment. All these examples are classic forms of "earned universalism": they get to a universal destination, but they do so by first addressing the barriers faced by members of marginalized groups. Put differently, the marginalized groups inspire social innovations that benefit all.

Lots of organizations already structure their equality initiatives around concepts with universal resonance. We've already mentioned allyship. Allyship initiatives help everyone, because everyone has advantages and disadvantages, which means everyone can benefit from having allies. An older white man who offers support to a younger woman of color when she experiences race or gender bias can receive support from her when he experiences ageism. To promote these win-win outcomes, we've worked with many organizations to create educational programs that teach people how to be better allies to each other.

Similarly, we've worked with other organizations to build programs around the concept of "authenticity" so that everyone who feels pressure to minimize or downplay outsider identities can be more authentic at school or work, whether they're an LGBTQ+ person of color or a white veteran from a rural area. Many common equality initiatives also strive to promote "psychological safety," management professor Amy Edmondson's term for a climate in which people feel safe to speak up and contribute their ideas without fear of punishment. Such initiatives clearly help workers who feel silenced because they belong to an underrepresented group, but a culture where people are freer to express themselves is also a culture that helps everyone.

A more universalistic approach to the project of equality—both in program design and in rhetoric—would defuse some of the most potent critiques of DEI. Many people across the political spectrum have argued that DEI obliterates individuality in favor of group identity. On the right, a report by the Heritage Foundation argues that members of the diversity movement "refuse to treat people as individuals" and instead "rely on discriminatory stereotypes and gross generalizations to label, judge, and group people based on race, gender, and ethnicity." The report's author, Jennifer Gratz, argues that "real diversity is found in the wealth of experience, talents,

STRATEGY 5: EMBRACE THE UNIVERSAL

perspectives, and interests of unique individuals." On the left, philosopher Susan Neiman argues that the progressive movement went awry when it turned away from "universalism" toward "tribalism." Instead of making appeals to our common humanity, Neiman argues, the left insisted on seeing people primarily through the lens of their group differences. And in the center, political scientist Yascha Mounk laments that "universalism has fallen out of favor," noting that "progressives have increasingly militated for the creation of spaces and organizations in which members of minority groups can remain among themselves." Mounk argues that such "progressive separatism" is more likely to lead to "destructive interethnic competition than it is to overcome the injustices of the past."

Opening up equality programs to all comers and emphasizing their universal benefits would largely take care of these objections. When an organization shifts its programs from "cohorts to content" or from "cohorts to character," it treats everyone as an individual, capable of contributing to the mission of each program based on their own values and life experiences. To use Gratz's language, the programs draw on the "wealth of experience, talents, perspectives, and interests of unique individuals" rather than judging people based on their race, gender, or ethnicity.

Although, as we've noted, universalism comes with costs, we genuinely admire the impulse to treat people more as individuals and less as monolithic group members. Psychologists have found that "individuation" is an important strategy for reducing prejudice and discrimination. Individuation is a mental habit of seeking specific information about, and focusing on, the personal characteristics of people from other groups so you avoid stereotyping them as homogeneous. In one study, researchers found participants primed to reflect on the "variability" within another social group (such as the different physical characteristics, attitudes, behaviors, ages, professions, and interests among Moroccan people, Chinese people, and Arab people) held less prejudiced attitudes toward, and discriminated less against, those groups than participants primed to view them monolithically. This finding makes sense: an underrepresented person, say a Middle Eastern student, is much less likely to be stereotyped if there's a critical mass of other Middle

Eastern students in the classroom. When you're the only representative of a group, you're at risk of becoming the spokesperson.

Who we are as human beings is a complex interplay of our group membership and individual character traits. It was a common perception that DEI over-indexed on group identity, causing people to view themselves and others primarily through their differences. As often happens when the pendulum has swung too far in one direction, the backlash has overcorrected, needlessly barring even sensible consideration of group-based remedies. But that backlash still leaves a pathway open for solutions that respect both our group and individual identities. Earned universalism lights the way down that broad and beckoning avenue.

STRATEGY 5 TAKEAWAYS

- The legal landscape has made it riskier for organizations to adopt "targeted programs" that reserve scholarships, grants, internships, fellowships, or other benefits specifically for underrepresented groups.

- Programs open to all can still advance the project of equality. We don't recommend "unearned universalism," which demands that people "unify" without acknowledging or addressing group inequalities. Instead, we recommend "earned universalism," which addresses group disparities on the path to achieving unity.

- One universal approach is to shift from "cohorts to content" to allow anyone to participate in a program so long as they're committed to the content of the program.

- Another universal approach is to shift from "cohorts to character" to allow anyone to participate so long as their life experience reflects strengths valued by the program.

- Earned universalism could help the project of equality move beyond a zero-sum game and emphasize the wide benefits of inclusive institutions.

Strategy 6:
RECLAIM MERIT

In 2025, the Michigan House of Representatives passed a bill requiring state agencies to hire employees based on merit. Michigan Republicans touted the measure as "anti-DEI legislation," stating: "There is no place for DEI in our government." Yet Michigan Democrats also supported the measure. Democratic Representative Erin Byrnes noted the legislation would "create opportunity by eroding the barrier of the old boys' club as we work toward a more equal playing field for all Michiganders." Speaking after the vote, Byrnes added: "House Republicans in Michigan voted yes on a DEI bill. I love that for them."

We applaud Byrnes's strategy of reclaiming the idea of merit. In our definition, assessing people based on "merit" refers to the simple yet profound idea of judging them based on their knowledge, competence, and skills. This definition of merit should be a friend to the project of equality. A major reason our society needs equality initiatives is to overcome a long history of unfairly assessing people based on criteria other than merit, such as their race or gender. Our work as equality advocates is to make sure these unfair biases don't prevent marginalized groups from being seen for their real potential. As inclusion consultant Emma McKee argues, "DEI is the true merit-based system."

Yet more often than not, it's the anti-DEI side that has leaned in to the concept, framing merit as somehow at odds with the project of equality. Executive orders from the Trump administration proudly claim to restore "meritocracy" and "merit-based opportunity" from the scourge of DEI. Prominent anti-DEI writer Heather Mac Donald states: "At present, you can have diversity, or you can have meritocracy. You cannot have both."

Unfortunately, instead of defending their work as merit-based, some of our allies feed the misconception that merit belongs to DEI opponents. Alison Collins, a former San Francisco Board of Education commissioner, argues that merit is "the antithesis of fair." Other diversity leaders have explicitly told us they have a visceral negative reaction to the term and urge equality advocates not to use it. As one of them said to us, "Any discussion of merit in the DEI context really chaps my ass."

It's long past time for advocates of the equality project to rethink their reticence and reclaim merit. Promoting merit has always been intertwined with promoting equality, and we need to make that connection clearer in the public debate.

THE STRATEGIC ARGUMENT FOR EMBRACING MERIT

It's dangerous to surrender merit to opponents of DEI, as the concept seems to have the country in its thrall. Research has shown that Americans tend to embrace meritocracy more than citizens of other countries.

A reminder of our nation's love affair with merit came in June 2024, when the CEO of Scale AI published a post that transformed the public conversation around DEI. His post introduced the concept of "MEI," defined as merit, excellence, and intelligence: "We hire only the best person for the job, we seek out and demand excellence, and we unapologetically prefer people who are very smart." The concept of MEI went viral. Elon Musk called it "great." Other corporate leaders like Shaun Maguire at Sequoia and Brian Armstrong at Coinbase also backed the concept. By March 2025, the term had become so popular that economics professor Roland Fryer observed: "DEI is dying. MEI is the new corporate rage."

The right response to these paeans to merit is to join the chorus ourselves, as Representative Byrnes did in the debates over the Michigan law.

We shouldn't cede the idea of merit to opponents of DEI. We should instead point out that diversity and merit go hand in hand. The Scale AI CEO himself explicitly rejected the notion that MEI conflicts with diversity, stating that "no group has a monopoly on excellence" and that "a hiring process based on merit will naturally yield a variety of backgrounds, perspectives, and ideas." The reason he might perceive a difference between MEI and DEI is that he appears to conflate DEI with race-based preferences. In defining MEI, the post states: "We will not pick winners and losers based on someone being the 'right' or 'wrong' race, gender, and so on." But if picking identity-based "winners and losers" is the definition of DEI, it's a stingy and misleading one.

It's also bad strategy to surrender the concept of merit, because it prevents us from forcefully challenging meritless decision-making by opponents of the equality project. As we've argued, suppression of free speech by equality proponents makes us seem hypocritical when we challenge suppression of speech by opponents. Denigrating merit operates in the same way. The Trump administration has signaled its unwavering commitment to meritocracy while also naming a weekend TV show host to lead the world's largest military, a professional wrestling executive to lead the Department of Education, and a man who embraces pseudoscience to lead the Department of Health and Human Services. Equality supporters will find it hard to express alarm about the qualifications (or lack thereof) of these individuals if we treat merit as an invalid concept.

Reclaiming merit also allows supporters of the equality project to demand that affirmative action opponents live up to their stated commitment to merit-based college admissions. When the legal nonprofit Lawyers for Civil Rights filed a complaint challenging donor and legacy admissions at Harvard, its executive director, Iván Espinoza-Madrigal, stated: "Your family's last name and the size of your bank account are not a measure of merit, and should have no bearing on the college admissions process." Had he relinquished the idea of merit, he would have relinquished this important argument.

PRINCIPLED CRITIQUES OF MERIT

In our experience, most equality advocates who critique merit do so on principled, rather than strategic, grounds. Their objections largely fall within three buckets—that merit is often subjective, unearned, or unduly instrumental. All three objections are weighty, and we wish to give them their due before turning to how they can be overcome.

First and foremost, critics say the concept of merit is highly subjective, which makes it essentially meaningless. In some areas, of course, merit is clear and objectively measurable: the most meritorious swimmer at the Olympics is the person who touches the end of the pool before the other swimmers. But we can't quarrel with the general idea that merit is often subjective. When hiring a teacher, you might look for someone with strong academic credentials, emotional intelligence, organizational skills, writing ability, patience, passion for the subject matter, or any number of other attributes. How you rank the importance of such characteristics is more complicated. And in some domains, the subjectivity of the assessment is even greater. How do you assess the best poet, pastor, or pianist?

Just because merit is debatable, however, doesn't mean it's incoherent. Even in choosing the best poet, pastor, or pianist, you're likely to find a stronger candidate through a merit-based process than through flipping a coin. In our own professional lives, when we've graded student papers together, we sometimes disagree about whether a student deserves an A-minus or a B-plus. But we almost always see a clear difference between an A paper and a C paper, whether due to the rigor of the analysis, the depth of the research, or the quality of the writing. On the rare occasions we don't, we can usually discuss our way to a consensus.

A narrower version of this critique is more convincing. This version doesn't say all merit is bunk. Rather, it says merit leaves a lot of discretion, so the dominant group that defines merit will abuse that discretion to favor itself. In an illuminating study, a sociologist tested the attitudes of white

Californians toward merit-based college admissions. Specifically, the researcher asked them to consider how much weight universities should place on high school grade point average (GPA) versus leadership and community service. The study found that white respondents were much more likely to emphasize GPA when primed to perceive Black students as their main competition for college slots. When primed to perceive Asian students as their main competition, GPA abruptly became less important. As the researcher observed, "this finding weakens the argument that white commitment to meritocracy is purely based on principle." Instead, people define merit differently depending on whichever definition will most advantage their own group against others.

This study is more than just an experiment. In the early twentieth century, many elite colleges changed their admissions processes to cap enrollment by Jewish students. They looked for geographic diversity to find students from states with low Jewish populations, introduced in-person interviews so admissions officers could more easily identify Jewish applicants, and assessed students on characteristics, such as "public spirit" and "leadership," thought to be more typical of Christians than Jews. These colleges manipulated merit to fence out students they deemed undesirable. Merit didn't define the favored group. The favored group defined merit.

In the choicest irony of all, scholars have identified a "paradox of meritocracy" where those who claim to be more committed to meritocracy often display more bias. In one study, researchers asked participants to assign bonuses to employees on behalf of a made-up company. When told the company assigned bonuses purely on merit, the participants were more likely to be biased in favor of men over equally qualified women. The researchers hypothesized that a "culture that prides itself on meritocracy may encourage bias by convincing managers that they themselves are unbiased." The same culture may then "discourage them from closely examining their own behaviors for signs of prejudice."

A second critique is that merit is often unearned. Factors like family connections or wealth make it much easier for some to develop capabilities than others. We've already mentioned that Americans fetishize merit. Yet research also shows Americans perceive merit-based assessments as unfair when obstacles hindered someone's ability to acquire the relevant qualifications. In one study, participants were told about a hiring committee focused on "getting the most qualified candidate" for a role. The committee chose one candidate, Jim, over another candidate, Tom, because Jim had better grades and loads of internships and extracurricular activities. When participants learned that Tom was just as hardworking as Jim but lacked the family support and resources to attend good schools, study without a part-time job, or complete unpaid extracurricular activities, participants rated the supposedly merit-based hiring decision as significantly less fair.

The third and final objection is that merit is unduly instrumental. By valuing what people can do, rather than who they are, merit scants their innate worth as human beings. The treatment of disabled people presents a vivid instance of how a society unduly fixated on merit can be dehumanizing. In his book *Disability Pride*, journalist Ben Mattlin makes an impassioned case for recognizing the equal dignity of individuals with disabilities. Mattlin was born with spinal muscular atrophy, a congenital muscle weakness. Reactions to his "soggy-hotdog arms" led him to be painfully self-conscious as a child. He drew solace from a seventeenth-century sonnet that John Milton wrote while going blind. The sonnet voices Milton's fear that he wasn't doing enough to serve God. But the sonnet then goes on to say that people don't need to give God "work" or "gifts." Rather: "They also serve who only stand and wait." Mattlin interprets this line as Milton "affirming that his existence still mattered, his life still had purpose." Mattlin took inspiration from this message: "It told me that my life mattered. I had purpose. It was, I think now, an early expression of disability pride." Both Milton's poem and Mattlin's book underscore that a society that prizes human beings only through their merit risks obscuring the inherent value of us all.

This point connects deeply with the values of the equality project. To their great credit, our allies in this movement believe all human beings deserve lives of dignity and opportunity, even as people differ markedly in their merit-based qualifications and skills. They tend to sympathize with individuals at the margins of society who don't meet traditional conceptions of merit, whether because of their disabilities, lack of educational or economic opportunities, or other barriers to success.

The charge that merit obscures our common humanity has been taken up far beyond the context of disability. In his book *The Tyranny of Merit*, philosopher Michael Sandel spotlights the dangers of the "meritocratic imperative—the unrelenting pressure to perform, to achieve, to succeed." Such pressure means even the people who have the genetic or environmental supports necessary to succeed in the meritocracy are run through a "high-stress, anxiety-ridden, sleep-deprived gauntlet" to emerge victorious. This imperative hurts not just individuals, but also society as a whole, because it cultivates a humiliating sense of failure among those who lose the meritocracy contest, and a smug, self-congratulatory attitude among the people who win it. This result fuels populist anger among society's "losers" and a high tolerance for inequality among its "winners." Sandel's insight neatly inverts the common critique that DEI is divisive because it creates a system of identity-based spoils. In Sandel's account, merit can also be divisive. Merit fractures communities into the worthy and the unworthy—communities that might otherwise find solidarity in their members' common humanity.

RECONSTRUCTING MERIT: A PRINCIPLED DEFENSE

Given these blistering critiques, why are we still fans of merit? Our central answer is what we call the "social reliance" argument. If you go to a doctor, you expect that they have gone to medical school and have the training to treat you with expertise that exceeds that of a layperson scanning WebMD. If you hire an accountant, you similarly presume they're competent to do your taxes, both in terms of their knowledge and qualifications. If you get on a plane, you trust the pilot can safely fly it, and that they've gone through hundreds of hours of training to earn that trust. When you use your microwave, boot up your computer, or cross a bridge, you assume it won't explode, electrocute you, or collapse under your feet. A well-functioning society requires such reliance, and to satisfy it, we need merit-based assessments.

Too often, this social reliance argument gets obscured because debates about merit focus on the person applying for the job, not on the people affected by the job they do. We should of course ensure aspiring physicians, accountants, and pilots are chosen through processes that aren't tainted by bias, don't unfairly favor people born on third base, and don't treat unsuccessful candidates as "losers" undeserving of social esteem. At the same time, we all count on society to offer us a basic level of competence.

A novel by Lionel Shriver imagines what happens when this social reliance interest is disregarded. In *Mania*, Shriver conjures a dystopian alternate timeline in which the "mental parity" movement has taken over the United States, ignited by a manifesto titled *The Calumny of I.Q.: Why Discrimination Against "Dumb People" Is the Last Great Civil Rights Fight*. The movement leads the country to become a toxic idiocracy. Cars blow up, people buy their food abroad to avoid being poisoned, and tens of millions of people die because a vaccine developer is unable to hire qualified scientists. The protagonist's partner, Wade, an arborist, is injured by an assistant he was forced to hire who knows nothing about the trade (including, as it happens, about how to operate a chainsaw). Because medical degrees are handed out like "shopping flyers," the physician who operates on Wade botches his ankle surgery. Nurses then almost kill him by giving him the wrong medication. Fortunately, a fifty-something doctor trained in the days before the mental parity movement is there to save him. Except for the old guard, this is a world in chaos, where no one can count on competence of any kind.

We view the social reliance argument as the bedrock of the case for merit. Embracing merit has its flaws. But just like the adage that democracy is the worst form of government except all the others, merit is the worst form of assessment except all the others. Think of the major alternatives, which include popularity, wealth, cronyism, nepotism, or a lottery system. In many domains, merit is clearly superior to these other options.

The social reliance argument, however, doesn't allow us to ignore the critiques that merit is subjective, that it's sometimes unearned, and that it's unduly instrumental. Each critique can guide us toward a more nuanced and humane vision of what merit means and how it should be used by proponents of equality.

First, advocates of merit should be eternally vigilant about how bias might seep into an assessment. Critics have produced compelling evidence that human beings are prone to distorting criteria of merit for prejudiced or self-serving reasons. That tendency is, obviously, a problem. The equally obvious response is to get rid of bias rather than to get rid of merit.

We've already discussed several ways to fix such biases, but a nonexhaustive list might include the following. Decision-makers could agree in advance on what qualifications are truly relevant to the role, and commit to looking for those qualifications through a structured process that reduces reliance on gut feelings like the "stranded-in-the-airport" test. They could assess candidates not in a "slice of time" (how someone did on a particular exam) but in a "stream of time" (how someone has done across their career). They could educate themselves about common biases, such as favoring socioeconomically advantaged candidates who complete unpaid internships or participate in resource-intensive activities like lacrosse, fencing, or crew. They could move away from what legal scholar Lani Guinier called a "testocratic" conception of merit to include other important attributes, like a person's ability to collaborate with others or their commitment to serving their community.

They could also consider how diversity can be a component of merit, rather than antithetical to or independent of it. Black patients have better health care outcomes when treated by Black physicians. Many argue boys would do better in school with more male teachers. The accuracy of clinical drug trials depends on a diverse group of participants testing the drug. Teams composed of people from diverse backgrounds will tend to be smarter and more innovative than homogeneous ones. These are just a few examples of how diversity can improve the merit of individuals, groups, and organizations.

Second, when merit is unearned, as it sometimes is, equality advocates can balance considerations of merit against considerations of fairness. Even in such cases, merit-based decision-making can still be necessary to preserve social reliance interests. A person with every genetic and social advantage doesn't *deserve* to be a doctor more than a person who lacks those advantages. The reason we still allow doctors to be chosen on merit isn't for the doctor, but for the patient. We don't want medical certificates to be like Shriver's "shopping flyers," because that outcome would shatter the trust that patients have in their physicians.

Yet it's absolutely valid for fairness considerations to temper what might otherwise be a relentless focus on merit. In the study involving the hypothetical candidates Jim and Tom, a pure merit-based process would favor Jim— the candidate with better grades, internships, and extracurricular activities. But a hiring manager might fairly pick Tom instead, who appears to have just as much potential as Jim but historically had less opportunity to fulfill that potential.

A report by education scholars and consultants Arthur L. Coleman and Jamie Lewis Keith discusses this balancing act in the context of higher education admissions: "Students are often considered both on the face value of their achievements and the barriers they scaled or on the manner in which they took advantage of the opportunities presented to them." They describe how one institution, Pomona College, conducts its assessment: "We have different expectations for different students: the exam scores from a daughter of two college professors are viewed in a different context than the scores from a first-generation college student who attended an underfunded high school."

Finally, equality advocates should respond to the point that merit is unduly instrumental by thinking about different areas in which merit matters more or less. We agree with critics that our entire society shouldn't be organized around the guiding principle of meritocracy. Public schools should admit all children within a given area, rather than limiting who can attend based on their intelligence or skills. Hospitals should treat patients based on need, not based on whether they "deserve" treatment because they've pursued a healthy lifestyle. Families and friendship groups should extend care and loyalty to their members, even (or especially) if someone in the group performs poorly in school or struggles in the job market.

We don't want or need to put merit at the center of human life. Instead, we claim more modestly that merit should play an important role in many common institutional decisions, like hiring, promotion, work assignments, grading, access to sought-after educational and professional opportunities, and conferral of awards and prizes. Some of meritocracy's strongest critics share this more chastened vision of merit. Even Sandel states: "There is nothing wrong with hiring people based on merit. In fact, it is generally the right thing to do." He observes that it's more efficient to match people to the jobs they're most competent to perform, and that it would be unfair to deny opportunities to the most qualified people.

Moreover, we don't see the world as cleanly divided into merit-based and egalitarian spheres. Most human endeavors have a hybrid quality. Athletic organizations for children's sports commonly distinguish between competitive leagues that select children for their ability and open leagues that emphasize fun for all. Even in employment—where merit-based decision-making is on its strongest ground—most of us recognize exceptions to the general rule. To expand economic opportunity for people with significant disabilities, many governments fund programs to match disabled workers to the business needs of employers. Such programs depart from a narrow, market-driven conception of which employees have the greatest merit, but they promote justice for people with profound disabilities who might otherwise struggle to find work opportunities. To give another example, a plumber who runs his own small business might hire his son as an apprentice, rather than conducting a global search for a protégé with the greatest plumbing skills. Few would object to this mild form of nepotism.

To sum this all up, the pro-equality side must reclaim merit not only for strategic reasons, but also for principled ones. The "social reliance" argument makes merit an unavoidable feature of a functioning society. Although some of our allies have valid qualms about merit, those qualms only help us find a more defensible form of that ideal. The solution is not to end merit, but to mend it.

WHAT IT LOOKS LIKE TO CHAMPION A MORE NUANCED FORM OF MERIT

Some organizations tie diversity to merit in this more affirming and expansive way. Bob Sternfels, head of the consulting firm McKinsey, defended his firm's approach to equality in 2025 by stating that McKinsey would "continue to boldly pursue both" diversity and meritocracy, because a diverse meritocracy "has been part of our values from the start," enabling the firm to hire people from a variety of backgrounds, including women and military veterans. Observing that the firm doesn't "guarantee equity in outcomes," Sternfels noted that "we do strive to ensure everyone has a fair shot to succeed in our meritocracy." We like this statement because it recognizes that equality practices enable more merit-based decision-making, not less. Pharmaceutical company Pfizer also explicitly links these concepts. The diversity page on its website is headed "Merit-Based Diversity, Equity, and Inclusion," and explains that the company's "culture of diversity, equity, and inclusion is based on merit—one where hard work, talent, and contributions drive success, and barriers to opportunity are removed."

Research supports the approach taken by McKinsey and Pfizer. In one study, researchers looked at participants' reactions to three messages in a fictitious company's diversity mission statement. One, which they called the "multiculturalism condition," emphasized an inclusive workplace that values people's differences. The second, which they called the "value-in-merit condition," stressed looking for "the most qualified individuals." The third, the "multicultural meritocracy condition," combined the two. It highlighted the value of difference *and* the desire to find the most qualified individuals. The researchers found that the multicultural meritocracy message was the most effective of the three messages. For white participants, it reduced the activation of negative racial stereotypes and increased their feelings of engagement at work compared with the pure multiculturalism condition. For people of color, it increased their feelings of psychological engagement at work compared with the value-in-merit condition. For both groups, it heightened their feelings of inclusion. The researchers concluded that an "explicit commitment to *both* racial diversity and merit in their diversity policies and mission statements, rather than a singular focus on one," would allow organizations to engage white employees and employees of color alike.

THE PRAGMATIC IMPERATIVE TO RECLAIM MERIT

This discussion leaves a fundamental question hanging: Is it actually possible to reclaim merit? In our conversations with equality supporters, we've noticed that the people most nervous about the strategy of reclaiming merit are often advocates for the Black or Latino communities. This fact has made us wonder whether we, who aren't members of these communities, are missing something.

The root of the unease in the Black and Latino communities seems to be based on the history of people selectively weaponizing merit to paint Black and Latino individuals as unqualified. Sharon, a chief inclusion officer at a major law firm, told us that while her work has "always focused on merit," the terms "merit" and "meritocracy" are almost never "invoked unless it's in the context of candidates of color, particularly Black and Hispanic individuals." She added: "It often becomes a coded way to question whether those individuals truly 'deserve' to be where they are." Sharon observed that this idea was particularly galling to her, because the data told "a very different story." At her firm, fewer than half of the white lawyers graduated from first-tier law schools, while almost four-fifths of its lawyers of color did. Similarly, all lawyers of color met the grade point average cutoff established by the firm, while white attorneys were often allowed to fall below that cutoff due to strong client ties or connections to influential partners. Sharon concluded that emphasizing merit "gives unnecessary oxygen to a narrative that implicitly questions the qualifications of diverse professionals, despite overwhelming evidence that they've had to clear a higher bar to get here."

Our first reaction to Sharon's comments was to pick up on her statement that she has "always focused on merit." If merit is on her side, then why not say so and insist that everyone in the firm play by the same rules? However, she seems to be making a deeper point—that the word is so corrupted that it can never be rehabilitated. Sharon appears to be saying: "You think you're being clever by expanding the definition of merit. But the other side's definition is so entrenched in the public consciousness that every time you utter the word 'merit,' you give power to our opponents."

Yet even this more nuanced argument doesn't persuade us. For social reliance reasons, we're never going to move past the idea of merit, as it's the grease that makes the wheel of society turn. Merit isn't a concept we can avoid. We also don't have a more neutral alternative to capture the same meaning.

At the end of the day, we all subscribe to the idea of merit, whether we express qualms about it or not. Consider debates about the acronym DEI. Some opponents of DEI say the letters stand for "Didn't Earn It." Proponents clap back that DEI stands for "Doubly Earned It" or "Definitely Earned It." The fact that the debate is over the meaning of "D" tells its own story. Opponents say DEI gives its beneficiaries an unearned advantage. Proponents say DEI's beneficiaries have had to overcome bias and structural barriers to occupy their role. But both sides share the view that "E" stands for "earned," which is an invocation of merit. In the broader debate over the project of equality, as here, "merit" is inescapable. Whichever side successfully claims merit will win this war of ideas.

So we end where we began, with a clarion call to reclaim merit. We need to tell a story about a nuanced form of merit, not surrender merit to opponents. After all, we have the better story to tell.

STRATEGY 6 TAKEAWAYS

- Opponents of the equality project falsely insist that "merit" and "DEI" are at odds. Supporters of the equality project should reclaim the concept of merit for strategic and principled reasons.

- Reclaiming merit is strategically wise. Merit is a popular concept, and surrendering merit prevents us from forcefully challenging meritless decision-making by opponents of DEI.

- Reclaiming merit is also justified by principle. A well-functioning society depends on merit-based decision-making so that all of us experience competence and expertise as we go about our daily lives.

- Critics point out that merit is subjective, unearned, and unduly instrumental. Nevertheless, it's possible to reconstruct a more nuanced version of merit that successfully responds to these critiques.

Strategy 7:
HIGHLIGHT THE RISKS OF RETREAT

When we opened our research center in 2016, some folks expressed surprise that a law school housed it. At the time, the field of DEI wasn't associated with the law, meaning such a center would more likely be located in a social sciences department or a business school.

All that skepticism evaporated in the wake of the Supreme Court's 2023 affirmative action decision, when waves of lawsuits started crashing over diversity programs. Suddenly it seemed like a brilliant idea to have a center devoted to DEI operating out of a law school. A word we'd rarely heard in DEI conversations started cropping up again and again: "risk." And by "risk," people usually meant getting sued by anti-DEI activists.

We jumped into action, launching an online tracker of all federal lawsuits touching on DEI to educate the public. We explained the law to nervous leaders in webinars, summits, and op-eds. We consulted with organizations, using a traffic-light system that coded their DEI programs as red (high risk), yellow (medium risk), and green (low risk). It felt like the crisis we didn't know we'd been training for.

As time went by, leaders started telling us that while they appreciated our legal guidance, a narrow focus on the law was missing other important risks associated with DEI policies. One CEO said he found the legal risks relatively easy to handle, as he could just ask his attorney to do an assessment. But how could he gauge the risk of the Trump administration canceling his company's government contracts, slapping his company with a punitive executive order, or launching a spurious investigation that would drain the organization's time and resources? Other leaders told us they were increasingly concerned about anti-DEI muckraking by right-wing activists and social media mobs. Comments like these led us to widen our aperture, helping organizations navigate both the legal and social risks of doing DEI.

Yet even this expanded lens quickly seemed insufficient. We came to worry that responding only to the risks of *doing* equality work neglected a whole set of risks of *retreating* from it. What of people of color, women, and LGBTQ+ people who'd feel betrayed by a retreat? What of the progressive consumers who might boycott? What about the laws and norms of other countries around the world? What of the declining morale among current employees or potential recruits?

Over time, we saw signs our worries were well founded. Many leaders began telling us that after announcing a retreat from some equality programs, the pushback from their own employees was so vehement that the organization had to scramble to "do something" to show those employees it still cared about inclusion. One survey of 750 American business leaders, conducted in April and May 2025, found that one in five companies that had earlier rolled back their diversity initiatives were "quietly reintroducing or expanding" those initiatives, "possibly under a new name."

Ultimately, we concluded that navigating these choppy waters required a balanced sense of the risks in all directions—from the "anti-DEI" side as well as from the "pro-DEI" side. But the media wasn't helping. Each news cycle seemed to carry a headline about an organization that "rolled back," "ditched," or "dropped" DEI. This created a perception that the project of equality was a huge risk. That perception made it seem like the people still pursuing equality work were engaged in brave (or perhaps foolhardy) defiance. By contrast, turning your back on equality seemed like the sensible and safe option.

Opponents of the equality project love this narrative. If they convince people that equality initiatives are legally and socially risky, the most obvious solution is to shut down those initiatives entirely. To regain control of the narrative and sustain the project over the long haul, supporters need to insistently highlight why a retreat is itself a risky endeavor. There are at least four major categories of such risk.

LEGAL RISKS

A few months after the Supreme Court changed the landscape for DEI, we asked a chief diversity officer of a major news organization about her relationship with the company's head lawyer—known as the general counsel or "GC." She told us: "Before the affirmative action ruling, the GC paid no attention to us and didn't have a clue what my team was working on. Now, he's hovering over me all the time and wants to review every project, every policy, every piece of communication we put out into the world."

This joined-at-the-hip dynamic is now common. When a relationship between a chief diversity officer and GC is strong, the diversity leader will often joke to us that the two of them are "best friends" because they "hang out all the time." When the relationship is strained, the diversity leader will groan about how the GC is standing in the way like a defensive lineman, blocking everything they want to do.

By and large, the GCs we speak with have a sophisticated understanding of the legal risks in this area. But many people who aren't legally trained and don't live and breathe this work every day tend to fixate on one specific hazard: the risk of getting sued by opponents of DEI. They read the screaming headlines about white men suing their employers for "reverse discrimination" and the conservative activist groups filing their own legal challenges to diversity initiatives, and they don't want to be the next organization in the firing line.

This worry about getting slapped with an anti-DEI lawsuit was already widespread in late 2023 and 2024, so you can imagine what happened in January 2025 after President Trump took office again and started assailing DEI with executive orders. Heads practically exploded from the perceived legal risk. Our phones rang off the hook, causing our heads to nearly explode as well.

The incessant chatter about anti-DEI lawsuits and President Trump's executive orders has given many people the impression that the only legal threat relating to the project of equality comes from the people who want to shut it down. It's true that there's been a significant uptick in lawsuits challenging diversity initiatives, often coming from white men who claim equality programs discriminate against them. But when we speak with lawyers who practice in this area, they tell us that most discrimination complaints against their organizations are still filed by people of color, women, and members of other historically marginalized groups, not by white men.

In 2025, our center fielded a survey with the gender equity think tank Catalyst to find out if our anecdotal impressions were correct. They were. Sixty-eight percent of corporate executives and 65 percent of legal leaders in our survey said moving away from diversity efforts would create *more* legal risk for their organization. The reason? Nearly two-thirds of such leaders said there was a greater risk of litigation from "traditional" plaintiffs like people of color and women than from "non-traditional" plaintiffs like white men.

This finding means that while engaging in some equality efforts can be legally risky, retreating from those efforts can be as well. Let's suppose that many years ago, your workplace invested in initiatives to promote gender equality. It expanded its outreach to find more qualified women candidates, removed gender bias from evaluation and promotion processes, conducted a pay equity audit to close gender pay gaps, and established a women's network (open to all) to create a more inclusive climate. Then, in response to legal and political pressure, it ripped those programs away. Now, women no longer feel welcome. They're treated unfairly in hiring, evaluation, and promotion processes. They're paid less than men for the same work. The fair and inclusive environment your organization worked hard to create has turned toxic. Guess what: as a result of retreating from the project of equality, your workplace is now more, not less, exposed to discrimination lawsuits.

Organizations also need to be mindful of different legal risks at the federal and state level. In 2025, Verizon agreed to end DEI policies so the Federal Communications Commission would approve its purchase of another

STRATEGY 7: HIGHLIGHT THE RISKS OF RETREAT

broadband company. That decision didn't go down well with California's Public Utilities Commission, whose approval Verizon needs to operate in that state. California Commissioner John Reynolds challenged Verizon to explain its retreat from DEI. When Verizon gave a vague response, Reynolds released a ruling chastising the company. He noted that the Commission "does not tolerate false statements" and that Verizon's rollback of DEI may involve "a direct conflict" with California's Public Utilities Code.

Organizations must, then, engage in a balancing act. You're not backing away from a cliff when you retreat from the project of equality. You're standing on a bridge. If you back away too far, you'll fall off the other side.

REPUTATIONAL RISKS

In the spring of 2023, a social media influencer posted a short video to her Instagram account as part of a paid promotion with Anheuser-Busch (the makers of Bud Light) for the basketball tournament "March Madness." Smiling behind several cans of Bud Light, she jokes: "I kept hearing about this thing called March Madness, and I thought we were all just having a hectic month, but it turns out it has something to do with sports. And I'm not sure exactly which sport, but either way it's a cause to celebrate." She then takes a swig of beer. The video is unremarkable except for the fact that the influencer, Dylan Mulvaney, is a transgender woman. This fact arises briefly in the video when Mulvaney refers to having recently celebrated "day 365 of womanhood."

The backlash was swift and unremitting. Prominent conservatives blasted Anheuser-Busch on social media. In a totally normal and temperate display, the singer Kid Rock posted a video to his Instagram firing a gun at cans of Bud Light. Two of the company's marketing executives were placed on leave. Bud Light's market share tumbled. Ever since then, the Bud Light incident has served as a supposed cautionary tale for companies that promote DEI. "Go woke, go broke" became a catch cry on the right.

The reputational risks of embracing DEI became even more salient in 2024 when social media activist Robby Starbuck began attacking companies for their "woke" DEI policies. Starbuck, who has a massive following across multiple platforms, started by targeting corporations that have a conservative customer base, like Harley-Davidson, Tractor Supply, and John Deere. After notching some wins, he expanded to more mainstream brands like Ford, Pepsi, and Walmart. His posts often highlight the diversity policies at the targeted companies and urge his followers to protest and boycott. "No more DEI departments, no more woke trainings, no more donations to woke causes, no more donations to Pride parades," he said in one video. Starbuck's name has come up many times in conversations we've had with diversity leaders. When we give presentations to clients, their legal and risk teams often require the materials well in advance so they can remove content that could be screen-grabbed and circulated out of context. No one wants to get Starbucked.

Again, the fear of incurring Starbuck's ire has eclipsed the significant reputational risks in the other direction. In January 2025, only a few days into President Trump's second term, the retailer Target released a statement that it would end its DEI goals, stop participating in "external diversity-focused surveys," change its "supplier diversity team" to "supplier engagement," and make other adjustments to its DEI strategy. This statement sparked a boycott from DEI supporters who felt the company had abandoned its values and customer base. An Atlanta megachurch pastor, Jamal Bryant, has led the effort alongside other activists, urging Americans to spend their cash elsewhere until the company reverses its decision. "We will break Target," Bryant insists. "We will break any company that doesn't honor our dignity while they are trying to take our dollar."

When we first heard about this boycott, we didn't immediately clock its impact. It wasn't until people in our lives who pay little attention to DEI (or to politics in general) started telling us that they "miss shopping at Target" that we realized the boycott was effective. Those comments drove us to look at the data, which also suggested the boycott was making a difference. Foot traffic to Target's stores dipped immediately after the boycott was announced and continued to decline for months. Its share price also dropped. One consumer research firm found in 2025 that the number of Americans who said they regularly shopped at Target had gone down 19 percent since 2021. On an earnings call in May 2025, the Target CEO acknowledged its declining sales were caused in part by consumer reactions to its change in DEI strategy. Advocates have also urged a national boycott of Amazon, Dollar General, McDonald's, Walmart, and other brands for their DEI rollbacks.

We don't want to overstate the risks here. Many companies that have retreated from diversity initiatives have continued to thrive financially, just as many companies that have maintained or expanded their diversity initiatives have. The point is that reputational risks exist in both directions, and vary significantly depending on an organization's constituents. Tractor Supply—a company headquartered in Tennessee whose customers likely lean rural, conservative, white, and male—should probably think differently about this topic than Nike, whose customers are likely younger, more urban, and more liberal.

Just as leaders turn to general counsel to assess legal risks, some are now turning to their communications and marketing leads to get advice on the social risks associated with DEI. While such risks sound amorphous, assessing them doesn't need to involve pure guesswork. One organizational consultant told us she'd worked with a company to poll nearly a million of its customers about their social attitudes. The poll discovered that the company's customers were largely progressive. This finding gave the company's leaders the confidence to tell anti-DEI activists to buzz off.

Overall, the available evidence suggests the reputational risk of retreating from the equality project is significant. A 2025 *Axios* Harris poll, which surveyed more than sixteen thousand adults to gauge the reputation of the most visible brands in the United States, found that while corporate reputation declined overall across the hundred companies tested, the companies that maintained their DEI commitments amidst the backlash saw their reputation scores rise. *Axios* concluded: "Unclear corporate values or a lack of conviction—most recently seen through mass DEI walk-backs—can hinder reputation."

It's not just consumers. In our research with Catalyst, which surveyed people who work for medium and large organizations in corporate America, we found that employees overwhelmingly supported the values underpinning the project of equality. They also widely approved of common initiatives under that umbrella, such as employee resource groups, efforts to create a more inclusive work culture, and programs intended to increase representation like internships, mentorship programs, and leadership training. A majority of respondents also indicated they were more likely to take a job with an organization that supported DEI and stay with their employer long term if it continued to uphold those values. On the flip side, we regularly hear from leaders and employees who report a loss of morale after their organization announces a retreat from equality initiatives. Indeed, a July 2025 survey found that 47 percent of companies that pulled back on DEI after the November 2024 election experienced "a decline in employee morale."

GLOBAL RISKS

In March 2025, U.S. embassies sent letters to a variety of foreign companies, demanding that those companies certify they don't operate any unlawful DEI programs. This certification requirement was a major plank of President Trump's executive orders, applying to companies that do contract work with the U.S. federal government. But some foreign leaders, especially in Europe, loudly objected to these requirements being imposed outside the United States.

France's gender equality minister Aurore Bergé called it "an attempt to impose a diktat on our businesses," adding that it was "out of the question that we will prevent our business from promoting additional social progress and social rights." Belgium's foreign minister, Maxime Prévot, said his country would "not go back a millimeter" on diversity efforts. The Spanish Labor Ministry was even more forceful, describing the letter as a "flagrant violation" of Spain's discrimination and diversity laws, and warning that companies aiming to comply with the U.S. embassy's directive would face investigation by the country's Labor Inspectorate.

On the other side of the North Sea, Transport for London—a local

STRATEGY 7: HIGHLIGHT THE RISKS OF RETREAT

government entity controlled by London's mayor—nixed a bid by consulting firm Accenture to work on a fifty-million-pound marketing campaign for the agency. Accenture had announced two months earlier that it was scrapping some of its DEI initiatives. Transport for London was not amused. It stated through a spokesperson: "We were unable to continue with [Accenture's] bid for our creative tender contract as they no longer met the criteria for diversity that we expect from all suppliers. We are proud to hold our suppliers to account, making sure they are aligned with our commitments on diversity and inclusivity to help expand opportunities across our supply chain and create equal opportunities for all."

While the Trump administration was prosecuting its all-out assault on DEI in early 2025, the Australian Parliament passed a major pro-DEI law. The legislation requires employers with five hundred or more employees to adopt three gender equality targets, at least one of which has to be numeric (such as a percentage target to increase women's representation). Organizations have three years to achieve or demonstrate progress against their chosen targets, and need to publicly report on that progress. This law looks like the mirror image of the Trump executive order. Both the Australian and U.S. requirements threaten companies with the loss of lucrative government contracts. But the U.S. order punishes pro-DEI activity, while the Australian law punishes anti-DEI activity.

This pro-DEI position goes beyond European or commonwealth countries. Brazil passed an Equal Pay Act in 2023 requiring large companies to publish salary transparency and remuneration criteria reports, featuring data on gender, race, ethnicity, nationality, and age inequalities. It also pushed in 2025 for "diversity" to be recognized globally as a key principle in sustainable investment. And in Japan, a 2025 Reuters survey of Japanese companies found that 77 percent of respondents planned to press forward with diversity efforts. As one observed: "DEI is a global trend. We don't see it necessary to change our direction just because one country's president is against it."

In short, even as the United States is backsliding on the project of equality, many other regions of the globe are maintaining or advancing that project.

Given this backdrop, global organizations that want to succeed in countries that support equality initiatives can't withdraw completely from DEI. Otherwise they could violate local norms, be deprived of government contracts, or even breach laws that require affirmative efforts to advance equality. At the very least, such organizations will need to do what a *Wall Street Journal* headline neatly summarized as the "new playbook" for global companies based in Europe: "'Anti-Woke' in the U.S., DEI at Home."

The push to advance diversity abroad should also give Americans pause before retreating too far from their own domestic equality efforts. Many U.S. organizations have a significant international footprint, and employ people who frequently interact across borders. Such organizations often care about fostering a global brand identity and a cohesive internal culture. Requiring progressive countries to "level down" to U.S. norms could damage the organization's global reputation and stoke discontent from leaders and employees abroad. These concerns led one organization we worked with—a global consumer products company—to "level up" instead. As one of their leaders put it to us: "We're known for being inclusive. Many people who work here say they joined us because of our commitment to diversity. We know we're taking a little more risk in the United States by keeping initiatives in place, but it's better for our global brand than forcing our European colleagues to pull back."

TEMPORAL RISKS

Americans are split on the value of DEI. But underneath the surface lurks a consistent generation gap. A diversity leader once told us that while the Boomers at her organization felt iffy about DEI, "the Gen Zers we recruit are basically wearing Black Lives Matter T-shirts underneath their suits." Another leader—referring to his Gen Z colleagues with affectionate vexation as "snowflakes" for their obsession with inclusion—acknowledged that their attitudes had pushed his organization to take the project of equality more seriously: "They may be snowflakes, but they're our snowflakes, so we have to look after them."

STRATEGY 7: HIGHLIGHT THE RISKS OF RETREAT

Polls bolster this impression. A 2023 Pew survey found workers under the age of thirty were the most likely age group to say that "focusing on increasing diversity, equity, and inclusion at work" was a good thing. Sixty-eight percent of such workers favored DEI compared with 52 percent of the oldest workers. Other polls repeatedly find such a skew. A 2024 Gallup poll found younger Americans were more likely than older Americans to believe it was important for businesses to promote DEI, and a 2025 UMass poll found younger Americans were the least likely to support ending DEI at the federal level.

Even as generations turn over, it's not inevitable that support for the project of equality will increase. Political winds can shift, and people can become more conservative as they age. But it's indisputable that the generations most supportive of DEI are also the generations gradually taking over institutions. Every raging blizzard, after all, begins with flurries of snowflakes.

Reflecting on the temporal big picture should help leaders make wiser decisions in heated cultural moments. In 2020, many leaders tried to read the zeitgeist and made snap decisions to join the DEI frenzy. These decisions weren't always well thought out. In hindsight, some leaders may have gotten caught up in the heat of the moment, making splashy promises and launching progressive programs that they're now sheepishly rolling back. As journalist Simone Foxman reported in March 2025, reflecting on the explosion of DEI activity in 2020: "In the fervor to capitalize on an unprecedented interest in racial justice, few paused to scrutinize which initiatives were working and which weren't, and how much corporate America should be involved at all. And they were quick to dismiss criticism, even by those who supported their goals."

Leaders who wince now at their knee-jerk reactions to the 2020 zeitgeist should ponder whether their current decisions to roll back equality initiatives could also look cringeworthy to their future selves. If you're one of these leaders, think about the person you want to be five or ten years from now. Do you want to look back and regret your reactive withdrawal from the project of equality? Or do you want to look back with pride that you remained stalwart in the defense of the values you hold dear?

THE DIFFERENCE BETWEEN RETREAT AND EVOLUTION

Our discussion so far may have given the impression that all of us confront a binary choice: retreat from DEI or stand firm. The reality is more complex. Many people, feeling pressure from both directions, are grasping for a third option that allows them to hold on to their values without inviting the ire of anti-DEI activists or politicians.

The most common approach in this category is a rebrand. Writing in 2025, reporter Callum Borchers noted that practicing DEI was "like getting into a speakeasy, except the key is to *not* say the magic words." Borchers elaborated that many organizations were "ditching the DEI acronym and applying a blander label, like 'employee engagement,' to similar programs." Other words like "belonging," "opportunity," and "culture" are rising in popularity. We're now waiting for a diversity role to be titled "discrimination law compliance officer" or "chief meritocracy officer," if not "status quo preservationist."

Some equality advocates have argued such nomenclatural shifts are unacceptable withdrawals from the project of equality. "You erase the word 'diversity,' and you erase me," as one colleague put it. We get where these advocates are coming from: it's hard not to feel suspicious when an organization changes overnight how it talks about its supposedly fundamental values. But when you look at the history of the movement, the project of equality has gone by many names. Over the decades that advocates have worked to make institutions more inclusive, they've adopted a variety of labels—affirmative action, equal opportunity, diversity management, diversity and inclusion, DEI, and more. Of particular note, an earlier wave of backlash to "affirmative action" under the Reagan administration prompted the field's rebrand to "diversity management." Shifts in language are a natural process of evolution in a field as dynamic and contested as this one.

Just as the language will shift, so too will the work of equality itself. This entire book has sketched the transformation, in both rhetoric and substance, that the project of equality must undergo over the coming decades. As frustrating as this moment may feel, it's unrealistic to imagine that the work of equality can be frozen in time. If the only available choices are to abandon DEI or stick rigidly to the practices of the past, many will choose abandonment. We must be adaptable to uphold the project.

In the end, this work will survive by persuading the skittish people in the middle of the room, who are deciding how to respond to the swirling DEI controversy, to hold on to two truths. One is that the risks of walking away from the project of equality are too high. The other is that an era of retrenchment need not cause an era of retreat. It can instead prompt a renewal, making the work better than before.

STRATEGY 7 TAKEAWAYS

- The public narrative frames the project of equality as risky, while making a retreat seem safe. Supporters need to highlight the significant risks of retreat.

- Withdrawing from the project of equality involves legal risks. Removing programs that create a fairer and more inclusive environment for marginalized groups increases the risk of lawsuits from those groups.

- A retreat also involves reputational risks. Many customers, employees, students, and other stakeholders feel alienated when organizations turn their backs on equality.

- Many countries are continuing to advance the project of equality through their own laws, regulations, policies, and norms. In an interconnected world, organizations ignore these global developments at their peril.

- The youngest generations are the most supportive of the project of equality, which increases the risk of retreat over time as they take over institutions.

CONCLUSION

The battle over the project of equality is often cast as one between opponents who yearn for the past and proponents who want to forge ahead into the future. This portrait is too crude. Proponents of equality, like ourselves, are also drawn deeply to the past. The contrast isn't between nostalgia and progress, but among different forms of nostalgia. That insight has profoundly shaped how we conduct our work.

THEIR NOSTALGIA

Derived from words meaning "homecoming" and "pain," the word "nostalgia" describes an intense longing for the past, a form of homesickness shifted from a location to an era of time. President Trump has won two elections with the promise to "Make America Great Again," suggesting the nation can be restored to a former glory from which it has tragically declined.

Part of that agenda clearly means returning to the status hierarchies of the past. This can be seen not just in the ruthless war on DEI, but also in a myriad of related initiatives intended to roll us back to an earlier, simpler time for dominant groups. The administration effectively ended the asylum process for all groups except white South Africans. It ordered a comprehensive review of Smithsonian museums and exhibitions to ensure they focus on the "greatness" of America and avoid "improper ideology." It ordered the restoration of Confederate statues, renamed army bases to conform with their original Confederate names, and rebranded a navy ship that previously honored gay civil rights activist Harvey Milk. It appointed Christian nationalists to key government roles. It sanitized (and in some cases scrubbed) references to slavery and prominent Black historical figures on government websites, and only reversed the whitewashing after public outcry. President Trump issued an executive order to promote "patriotic education" and to crack down on so-called "discriminatory equity ideology" in schools. He took over the Kennedy Center for the Performing Arts to move it away from "woke culture."

Often, this project of nostalgia doesn't return America to the way things were, but rather to a sepia-toned fiction. For centuries, the tallest mountain in North America was known as Denali. In 1896, a gold prospector renamed it Mount McKinley for a presidential candidate he admired. In 2015, President Barack Obama changed the name back to Denali. Yet President Trump styled an executive order renaming Denali "Mount McKinley" as "Restoring Names that Honor American Greatness." This formulation distorts the idea of "restoration"—President Obama had a greater claim to restoring the original name than President Trump did. The aim here isn't accurate representation, but a return to a once-upon-a-time past where currently dominant groups were even more in charge.

As this nostalgia often takes "colorblindness" as its calling card, we're reminded of an oddity in the iconography of justice. As we all know, justice is often figured as a blindfolded woman holding scales—the blindfold symbolizing her impartiality. What's less well known is that representations of justice also historically included an ostrich. Because the ostrich is fabled for burying its head, this usage led critics to ridicule it as a symbol of justice's stupidity. No surprise, then, that the ostrich has been retired.

Yet our opponents' nostalgia would resurrect the ostrich. It asks us to forget that the Constitution protects the "free exercise" of every religion, not just Christianity. It asks us to forget that Native American greatness is also American greatness. And it asks us to forget that an American history that elides the Black experience isn't history, but fantasy.

OUR NOSTALGIA

It would be a mistake, however, to believe opponents of the equality project are merely hidebound and regressive, while we are solely focused on the future. Proponents of equality are nostalgic too. There is nostalgia in our movement's reverence for the Supreme Court's ringing statement that separate is "inherently unequal" in *Brown v. Board of Education*, or the federal Constitution's guarantee of "equal protection," or the Declaration of Independence's statement, however incomplete, that "all men are created equal." Casting ourselves as the people who only look forward is a huge mistake because it's a huge deprivation. If anything, our movement should be more nostalgic than we are. We must find strength in the past, in all our forebears who fought for this project of equality before us. It's not that we should want to go back to those earlier points in history, when countless people suffered and died in conditions of horrifying injustice. Rather, we should aim to recapture the storied and honorable ideals that animated people to challenge that injustice.

We're dismayed that organizational equality work today isn't perceived as part of that history, but is instead seen as technocratic and trivial. As columnist Jamelle Bouie points out, for many people the term "DEI" conjures "HR mandates and ineffectual diversity training." If we were to ask instead what phrases like "civil rights" or "constitutional rights" evoke, the associations would reverberate in a deeper register—the register of our collective dignity and humanity. You might think of the Seneca Falls Convention that led to women's suffrage, or Dr. Martin Luther King Jr.'s "I Have a Dream" speech, or the Supreme Court decision that recognized nationwide marriage equality.

This disconnect is particularly tragic because the currently devalued work and the historically revered work are close relatives. In fact, civil rights law gave birth to the field of DEI. Proponents of equality should feel nostalgia for the vision that President Lyndon Johnson articulated when he signed the landmark Civil Rights Act of 1964 into law, observing that "those who are equal before God shall now also be equal in the polling booths, in the classrooms, in the factories, and in hotels, restaurants, movie theaters, and other places that provide service to the public." Johnson recognized that the value of equality couldn't just be an abstraction. It needed to have an institutional life across America to make the promise of civil rights real. That's exactly the work that members and leaders of organizations have done for decades through the project of equality.

So if you're a volunteer at your child's school developing resources to educate teachers about your nationality, you're a warrior for equality. If you're a student at a university advocating for greater disability accommodations, you stand in a civil rights tradition that dates back at least to the 1973 Rehabilitation Act. If you're an employee at your workplace trying to set up a new interfaith affinity group, you stand in a human rights tradition at least as old as the Constitution. These actions aren't as grand as arguing a voting rights case in front of the Supreme Court or passing a law through Congress. Yet this is the everyday work that makes our institutions live up to the ideal of equal opportunity for all. It's what makes equality vivid, what makes it daily, and, ultimately, what makes it matter.

THE FUTURE OF NOSTALGIA

Our nostalgia tells us that our work today should be informed by the core insights of past equality movements. Supporters of equality will obviously disagree about what lessons to draw from those movements. We ourselves are nostalgic for two features of this history, which we think of as the sense and sensibility of the equality project. These two features have strongly influenced our strategies in this book, as well as our professional work more broadly.

First, the project of equality has historically benefited from rugged good sense. In the utopia of our dreams, we wouldn't have to worry about a conservative supermajority Supreme Court constraining the work of equality, or nativist political movements undoing social progress, or public opposition to practices like affirmative action. We could just philosophize about the ideal theory of equality and then push it out into society. Yet we're much more interested in engaging with the world as it actually is.

Supporters of equality can learn from Thurgood Marshall and his colleagues' brick-by-brick strategy to overturn *Plessy v. Ferguson*—the notorious 1896 Supreme Court decision that said "separate" facilities for Black and white individuals could be "equal." Obviously, Marshall disagreed with that decision, but he knew he couldn't immediately overturn it. So he filed lawsuits that gradually tightened the perimeter within which "separate" would count as "equal." He won a series of cases that said schools couldn't meet the "separate but equal" requirement through tricks, like sending Black students out of state to an "equal" facility, or shunting Black students to a school built hastily in the same state, or having Black students in the same school sit in different areas of the classroom or library. Only after winning these stepping-stone cases did he ask the court to overrule *Plessy*, which it did in *Brown*, fifty-eight years after *Plessy* was decided. Marshall's pragmatic, decades-long strategy became a template for then-lawyer Ruth Bader Ginsburg (among others) in fighting for gender equality, and for lawyer Mary Bonauto (among others) in fighting for marriage equality.

Marshall could easily have dug in his heels and just cried out that *Plessy v. Ferguson* was wrong. He would, of course, have been right. But that would have been scant help to the individuals whose rights he was seeking to vindicate. He recognized he needed to argue within real constraints rather than just having the correct moral convictions. We're all the better for it.

Aside from pragmatism, another way we hope equality supporters rediscover the "sense" of previous equality movements is by recommitting to persuasion. Advocates for equality throughout history have understood that the people who wish to change the status quo carry the burden of persuading others. Consider Sojourner Truth's speech asking "Ain't I a Woman?", or Frederick Douglass's "What, to the Slave, Is the Fourth of July?", or Betty Friedan's *The Feminine Mystique*, or Jonathan Rauch's careful argument in *Gay Marriage*, or Eric Garcia's memoir on autism, *We're Not Broken*. Our arguments and ideals are stronger and truer than those of our opponents. It's time we acted like it.

As part of that recommitment to persuasion, supporters of the equality project need to realize we have no choice but to engage with people who disagree with us, inspired by classical liberal values like tolerance and free speech. We're on the side of the disadvantaged and marginalized, which means we rarely have the power to achieve our goals through brute political force. There's of course a hallowed history of using blunt methods like demonstrations, callouts, walkouts, and sit-ins to shock people out of complacency and impel leaders to make systemic change. These are the methods that social psychologist Dolly Chugh calls "heat." Yet as Chugh points out, effective social movements also require "light"—meeting people where they are, persuading doubters through personal stories and reasoned argument, patiently engaging with opponents. Light is especially necessary in organizations, where people have long-lasting relationships as colleagues, students, friends, and neighbors. These are the spaces where people owe one another the respect of trying to persuade them. Relatedly, these are the spaces where they're most likely to be effective in doing so.

As much as we long for the "sense" of past equality movements, we also long for their "sensibility," by which we mean the core emotions that drove equality advocates to do what they did. One form of sensibility is the ineradicable hope that our forebears carried with them, even in times of despair. These days, cynicism is fashionable. It can seem intellectually and morally superior to believe that powerful groups are incorrigibly corrupt and that society can't improve through collective effort. But as psychologist Jamil Zaki observes in his book *Hope for Cynics*, cynicism is "a tool of the status quo." It prompts people to sit out elections, refrain from protest, and disengage from one another. Why bother trying to change the unchangeable?

Our forebears categorically rejected this cynical path. In the 1970s, the iconic labor activist Dolores Huerta wanted to challenge a law in Arizona that prohibited farmworkers' ability to boycott and strike. Trying to organize against the law, Huerta kept encountering resistance from people she tried to recruit: "Oh, here in Arizona you can't do any of that. In Arizona *no se puede* (no, you can't)." Huerta responded: "No, in Arizona *sí se puede* (yes, we can)!" That simple phrase—*sí se puede!*—became the slogan of Huerta's campaign, and continues to inspire political and social movements for equality decades later. Whether it's Huerta's rousing declaration, Harvey Milk's statement that "hope will never be silent," or Dr. King's exhortation to "accept finite disappointment, but never lose infinite hope," the great leaders of the past refused to give in to fatalism. We should refuse too.

Another form of sensibility that inspires our nostalgia is the moral passion that equality leaders brought to their work. Today, many people who work professionally on the project of equality, like chief inclusion officers, make a "business case" for their programs. They argue that creating a diverse and inclusive organizational culture promotes innovation, enhances the student learning experience, and increases corporate profits. We don't discount such instrumental justifications—they're important methods of achieving buy-in for equality efforts, especially in the private sector.

Yet we routinely notice that these justifications are not what really drive our colleagues, leading to what we call "reverse hypocrisy." If ordinary hypocrisy involves offering up noble motives to hide more venal ones, reverse hypocrisy is the opposite. Diversity professionals publicly emphasize—and believe in—the business case, but often privately admit the deeper reason they do this work is to promote fairness, justice, and the inherent dignity and equal worth of all human beings. When we ask them, they regularly share a personal story of how they became passionate about equality—being teased for their minority religion, feeling shame at school for being poor, battling racism or sexism in their career, having a transgender brother or sister, or parenting a disabled child. Looking back at earlier equality movements, we see countless leaders speaking with stirring emotional conviction about their causes. We think it's time for all who work on organizational equality efforts to express more clearly and from the heart what really motivates them.

We try to do so ourselves. Over these pages, we've made intellectual arguments for our equality strategies, grounded in our expertise as lawyers and scholars. We stand behind those arguments and want them to be assessed on their merits. Yet we'd like to end by taking our own advice and explaining why we care so intensely about the project of equality, and why we remain hopeful about its long-term future.

We're both the enormous beneficiaries of the push for equality. Despite the generation that separates us, we both grew up in an era where some U.S. states criminalized same-sex sexual activity, and where being gay was openly stigmatized. Same-sex marriage was illegal well into our adulthood. Social mores and laws strongly discouraged, and sometimes prohibited, the formation of gay families. It's thanks to the ideal of equality that many of these injustices have been alleviated in our lives, at least for now.

For us, equality isn't an abstraction. We hear it in the laughter of our children when they rowdily wake us in the morning, and feel it in the embrace of our spouses at the end of the work day. It's the primal force that's changed our lives beyond the imagination of our younger selves. For that reason alone, equality has earned our eternal fealty. We'll fight for the ideal of equality for ourselves and others for the rest of our lives. We hope you will as well.

So we can't attack opponents of the equality project for experiencing nostalgia. We're just as nostalgic, but in a different way. We're nostalgic for the hard-headedness and soft-heartedness we associate with classical civil rights movements, their sober pragmatism combined with hope and passionate conviction. We believe those qualities allow the equality project to survive in any generation, whatever assaults come its way.

If the symbol of our opponents is the ostrich, our symbol is the phoenix. According to legend, the phoenix immolates itself in every era, only to be reborn from its own ashes. It's a potent image of hope and renewal in the face of adversity. Looking out at the state of the nation right now, we agree with our distressed colleagues that the equality project is engulfed in flames. But remember: we've seen this conflagration before. It's the burning that must take place before the new incarnation of equality arises. Equality endures because equality changes. That is how equality wins.

ACKNOWLEDGMENTS

Thanks to the many colleagues and partners in our work at NYU School of Law who have supported us and informed our thinking on the subject of this book. Dean Troy McKenzie has been a wonderful champion of our center through all the ups and downs of the past few years. We also thank Ashley Berry, John Brophy, Shirley Dang, Mindy Darwish, Bao Dinh, Christine Gagnon, Chihiro Isozaki, Christina Thomas, Claire Whitman, and the many sponsors of the Meltzer Center. A special shout-out goes to Roger Meltzer, after whom our center is named, for his stalwart support.

We were fortunate to work with an abundance of stellar research assistants at NYU Law and beyond. Deep thanks go to each and every one of them for their tireless efforts: Nicole Arslanian, Stuart Baum, Rafaella Cattani, Yejin Chang, Aarya Chidambaram, Darin DaCosta, Mer Fagliano, Vico Fortier, Gwendolyn Strasberg Gardner, Sebastian Hartley, Alexis Julien, Zachary Kasdin, Yashica Kataria, Chloe Kellison, Maya Konstantino, Melanie Lee, Nia McFall, Tiffany Namkoong, Bex Rothenburg-Montz, Fritzie Schwentker, Langley Seibert, Morgan Smith, Mia Song, Rachel Stewart, Olivia Turk, Charlotte Varcoe-Wolfson, Ashni Verma, Sam Vitale, Sammy Wang, Donna Webster, and Adela Zhou.

During the writing process, we asked a trusted group of early readers to give us feedback on a draft of the manuscript: Yasmin Abdullah, Adam Dixon, Rebecca Dixon, Maggie Frank-Hsu, Christine Gagnon, Andrew Glasgow Perez, Christina Joseph, Sam Lalanne, Betsy Lerner, Alixandra Pollack, Susan Reid, Ron Stoneham, and Alisha Stoun. We thank each of these early readers for taking time out of their busy schedules to help us improve our work. We also thank the participants at a forum we hosted in July 2025 who offered us candid feedback on our ideas and shaped the direction of the manuscript.

The team at Simon Acumen championed this book from the outset. This is the second time we have worked with our wonderful editor Stephanie Hitchcock, who showed us again why she is such a deeply respected name in this field. Thank you, Stephanie, for bringing such passion and purpose to your work, and for ensuring we do the same. Many thanks also to the rest of the excellent team at Simon Acumen, including Richard Rhorer, Will Scarlett, Elizabeth Breeden, Jessica Preeg, Karina Leon, and the terrific copyediting and art departments.

Finally, we thank our incredible agent, Betsy Lerner, for her wise counsel from the moment we hatched the idea for this book through to the final manuscript. Betsy is everything we would want an agent to be and more.

ADDITIONAL ACKNOWLEDGMENTS FROM KENJI

I want to begin by thanking my coauthor, David, for once again being such a wise, kind, and indefatigable collaborator for our second book together. I thank my agent and advisor, Christine Gagnon, and her colleague John Brophy, for the all-important work of keeping the world at bay while we wrote this book on a tight timeline. For similar reasons, I thank the Filomen D'Agostino and Max E. Greenberg Faculty Research Fund of NYU School of Law for generous research support. I am grateful to the brilliant Ina Bort, who is my favorite person to talk books with, and her superhumanly strong and compassionate spouse, Cathy Sharkey—you will both know why I'm singling you two out on this round. I thank friends, colleagues, teachers, and students too numerous to mention, with the faith that they will all know who they are.

My deepest thanks, as always, go to my family—my husband, Ron; my daughter, Sophia; and my son, Luke. That family also includes my parents, Michael and Chiyoko Yoshino; my sisters-in-law Donna Stoneham and Julie Nestingen; and my sister Kaye Yoshino. That family somehow now includes two nonhuman members—provoking an astonishment that takes nothing away from my affection—Great Dane Lucy and corn snake Theo. I hope you never forget how much each and every one of you mean to me; I know I never do.

ADDITIONAL ACKNOWLEDGMENTS FROM DAVID

My first thanks go to my coauthor, Kenji. It was again such a joy to collaborate with you on this project. I also want to thank Chloé White, our kids' nanny, for enabling me to devote so much time to writing this book on a compressed schedule. I have a wonderful family back home in Australia—my parents, Kim and Clive; my sister Claire; as well as my brother-in-law Michael and nephews Maddox and Gabe. I miss you every day and wish we all lived closer. Finally, I'd like to thank my sons, Hugo and Theodore, and my husband, Andrew. Thank you for encouraging me throughout the writing process and for being such compassionate and kind human beings. I love you and am forever grateful to have such a beautiful family.

ADDITIONAL LEGAL RESOURCES

Many of the strategies in this book are informed by our understanding of the legal landscape for equality work. For a deeper dive into the law in this area, as well as guidance on how organizations can navigate risk, we recommend the following additional reading:

- Advancing DEI Initiative (website), https://advancingdei.meltzercenter.org/
- Kenji Yoshino and David Glasgow, "What SCOTUS's Affirmative Action Decision Means for Corporate DEI," *Harvard Business Review*, July 12, 2023, https://hbr.org/2023/07/what-scotuss-affirmative-action-decision-means-for-corporate-dei
- Kenji Yoshino and David Glasgow, "DEI Is Under Attack. Here's How Companies Can Mitigate the Legal Risks," *Harvard Business Review*, January 5, 2024, https://hbr.org/2024/01/dei-is-under-attack-heres-how-companies-can-mitigate-the-legal-risks
- Kenji Yoshino and David Glasgow, "New Paradigm Shifts DEI from Box-Checking to Mindset-Building," *Bloomberg*, June 11, 2024, https://news.bloomberglaw.com/us-law-week/new-paradigm-can-shift-dei-from-box-checking-to-mindset-building
- Kenji Yoshino and David Glasgow, "The Irresistible Force and the Immovable Object: *Students for Fair Admissions* and Workplace DEI," *American Journal of Law and Equality* 4 (2024): 178–200, https://direct.mit.edu/ajle/article/doi/10.1162/ajle_a_00067/125066/THE-IRRESISTIBLE-FORCE-AND-THE-IMMOVABLE-OBJECT

ADDITIONAL LEGAL RESOURCES

- Kenji Yoshino, David Glasgow, and Christina Joseph, "What Trump's Second Term Could Mean for DEI," *Harvard Business Review*, November 14, 2024, https://hbr.org/2024/11/what-trumps-second-term-could-mean-for-dei?ab=HP-hero-latest-text-1
- Kenji Yoshino and David Glasgow, "Steer Clear of 'Illegal DEI' with Leveling—Not Lifting—Programs," *Bloomberg*, February 10, 2025, https://news.bloomberglaw.com/us-law-week/steer-clear-of-illegal-dei-with-leveling-not-lifting-programs
- Kenji Yoshino, David Glasgow, and Christina Joseph, "The Legal Landscape Around DEI Is Shifting. Your Messaging Should, Too," *Harvard Business Review*, February 11, 2025, https://hbr.org/2025/02/the-legal-landscape-around-dei-is-shifting-your-messaging-should-too?ab=HP-hero-latest-text-2
- Alixandra Pollack, David Glasgow, Tara Van Bommel PhD, Christina Joseph, and Kenji Yoshino, *Risks of retreat: The enduring inclusion imperative*, June 2025, Catalyst and Meltzer Center for Diversity, Inclusion, and Belonging, https://www.catalyst.org/insights/2025/risks-of-retreat-report

NOTES

INTRODUCTION

1. *On January 29, 2025*: Emily Shapiro, "DC plane crash live updates: Investigators comb through wreckage for clues," ABC News, February 6, 2025, https://abcnews.go.com/US/live-updates/dc-plane-crash-live-updates-salvage-operations/?id=118393207.
2. *When President Donald Trump took the podium*: Isaac Arnsdorf, "Trump baselessly blames diversity program for fatal air collision," *Washington Post*, January 30, 2025, https://www.washingtonpost.com/politics/2025/01/30/trump-dei-plane-crash/.
3. *Yet the newly re-elected leader*: Zeke Miller and Chris Megerian, "Trump blames diversity hiring as probe into deadly DC plane crash begins," Associated Press, January 30, 2025, https://apnews.com/article/trump-crash-reagan-washington-buttigieg-diversity-biden-ef1e07684bbc845e9e7981c1ae060af2.
4. *The aviation system*: Martin Pengelly, "Trump baselessly blames DEI and Democrats for Washington DC plane crash," *The Guardian*, January 30, 2025, https://www.theguardian.com/us-news/2025/jan/30/trump-washington-dc-plane-crash-dei.
5. *When the Francis Scott Key Bridge*: Anthony Sabatini (@AnthonySabatini), "DEI did this," X, March 26, 2024, https://x.com/AnthonySabatini/status/1772643640843604097?s=20.

NOTES

1. *As wildfires tore through*: Elon Musk (@ElonMusk), "DEI means people DIE," X, January 8, 2025, https://x.com/elonmusk/status/1877224004680843539.
2. *On the first day*: Exec. Order No. 14151, 90 Fed. Reg. 8339 (January 29, 2025).
2. *He followed with a barrage*: Exec. Order No. 14168, 90 Fed. Reg. 8615 (January 30, 2025); Exec. Order No. 14185, 90 Fed. Reg. 8763 (February 3, 2025); Exec. Order No. 14173, 90 Fed. Reg. 8633 (January 31, 2025).
2. *She stated her mission*: Kristen Parisi, "Senate Judiciary Committee holds hearing focusing largely on DEI rebrands," *HR Brew*, July 28, 2025, https://www.hr-brew.com/stories/2025/07/28/senate-judiciary-committee-holds-hearing-on-dei-focusing-largely-on-dei-rebrands.
2. *Lucas pledged to immediately*: Emma Colton, "'Unlawful DEI-motivated' workplace discrimination to be rooted out by Trump's new acting EEOC chair," Fox News, January 21, 2025, https://www.foxnews.com/politics/unlawful-dei-motivated-workplace-discrimination-rooted-out-trumps-new-acting-eeoc-chair.
2. *One of Trump's executive orders*: Exec. Order No. 14173, 90 Fed. Reg. 8633 (January 31, 2025).
2. *Not to be outdone*: Kristen Parisi, "DE&I leaders sue the Trump administration, while Attorney General Pam Bondi threatens criminal investigations," *HR Brew*, February 6, 2025, https://www.hr-brew.com/stories/2025/02/06/de-and-i-leaders-sue-the-trump-administration-while-attorney-general-pam-bondi-threatens-criminal-investigations.
2. *As the months rolled on*: Exec. Order No. 14319, 90 Fed. Reg. 35389 (July 28, 2025); Exec Order No. 14253, 90 Fed. Reg. 14563 (April 3, 2025).
3. *Lots more engaged in*: Jeff Green, "How Trump Reshaped Corporate DEI," *Bloomberg*, April 30, 2025, https://www.bloomberg.com/news/articles/2025-04-30/how-trump-has-reshaped-dei-in-corporate-america.
3. *In 2023, the court issued*: Students for Fair Admissions, Inc. v. President & Fellows of Harvard Coll., 600 U.S. 181 (2023).

3. *Specifically, the court signaled*: Jack Balkin and Reva Siegel, "The American Civil Rights Tradition: Anticlassification or Antisubordination?," *University of Miami Law Review* 58, no. 9 (2003).

3. *In the words of*: Adarand Constructors, Inc. v. Peña, 515 U.S. 200, 245 (1995).

3. *In its 2023 decision*: Jack Balkin and Reva Siegel, "The American Civil Rights Tradition: Anticlassification or Antisubordination?," *University of Miami Law Review* 58, no. 9 (2003).

4. *In fact, the court*: Ames v. Ohio Department of Youth Services, 145 S. Ct. 1540 (2025).

4. *Smelling blood in the water*: Advancing DEI Initiative (website), accessed September 4, 2025, https://advancingdei.meltzercenter.org/.

4. *Even progressives began to turn*: See, e.g., Jennifer C. Pan, *Selling Social Justice: Why the Rich Love Antiracism* (New York: Verso, 2025); Robert Kuttner, "The Corporate Capture of DEI," *The American Prospect*, October 24, 2023, https://prospect.org/power/2023-10-24-corporate-capture-of-dei/.

4. *Some commentators drew*: See, e.g., Howard Tullman, "Here's Why I Think DEI Is Dead," *Inc.*, July 30, 2024, https://www.inc.com/howard-tullman/heres-why-i-think-dei-is-dead.html; Joel Kotkin, "DEI is dead. The establishment media just doesn't want you to know it," *The Telegraph*, November 29, 2024, https://www.telegraph.co.uk/us/comment/2024/11/29/dei-dead-why-trump-election-will-accelerate-death-diversity/.

5. *The work of every generation*: Both sides of the ideological spectrum often regard the liberal narrative of American history as reflecting this story of gradual progress. See, e.g., Matthew Rose, *A World After Liberalism* (New Haven: Yale University Press, 2021), 4. ("Feminism, marriage equality, racial justice, multiculturalism—the left governed political life by controlling how we imagined the arc of history. It convinced Americans that history progressed by removing barriers to inclusion and equality.") We also thank Stacey Abrams for making the same point from a liberal perspective at a private in-person event.

5. *More recently, the murder*: Larry Buchanan, Quoctrung Bui, and Jugal K. Patel, "Black Lives Matter May Be the Largest Movement in U.S. History," *New York Times*, July 3, 2020, https://www.nytimes.com/interactive/2020/07/03/us/george-floyd-protests-crowd-size.html.

5. *Some proclaimed this head-spinning change*: See, e.g., Jonathan Chait, "The Great Awokening Is Over, But Trump Might Revive It," *New York Magazine*, June 26, 2024, https://nymag.com/intelligencer/article/donald-trump-joe-biden-great-awokening-george-floyd.html.

6. *Multiple public opinion polls*: See, e.g., Taylor Telford, Emmanuel Felton, and Emily Guskin, "Most Americans approve of DEI, according to Post-Ipsos poll," *Washington Post*, June 18, 2024, https://www.washingtonpost.com/nation/2024/06/18/affirmative-action-dei-attiudes-poll/; Rachel Minkin, "Views of DEI have become slightly more negative among U.S. workers," Pew Research Center, November 19, 2024, https://www.pewresearch.org/short-reads/2024/11/19/views-of-dei-have-become-slightly-more-negative-among-us-workers/; Doug Rice et al., "New research shows the American public continues to support diversity, equity, and inclusion policies," *London School of Economics and Political Science* (blog), June 4, 2025, https://blogs.lse.ac.uk/usappblog/2025/06/04/new-research-shows-the-american-public-continues-to-support-diversity-equity-and-inclusion-policies/.

6. *Even when Americans express*: Terry Tang and Amelia Thomson-Deveaux, "Fewer Americans see discrimination as anti-DEI push gains traction, AP-NORC poll shows," Associated Press, July 31, 2025, https://apnews.com/article/poll-dei-diversity-equity-inclusion-discrimination-7b285f32b2e1f4e95a86f5ecaf130774.

6. *A Siena College Research Institute*: Travis Brodbeck et al., "Beyond DEI: Understanding Public Opinion on Diversity, Equity, & Inclusion," *American Association for Public Opinion Research*, March 20, 2025, https://aapor.org/newsletters/beyond-dei-understanding-public-opinion-on-diversity-equity-inclusion/.

6. *An Axios poll*: Emily Peck, "Americans are fine with corporate DEI,"

Axios, January 17, 2025, https://www.axios.com/2025/01/17/diversity-initiatives-workers-trump.

6. *The Heritage Foundation*: Jonathan Butcher, "Corporations Are Finally Giving DEI the Pink Slip," The Heritage Foundation, December 6, 2024, https://www.heritage.org/civil-society/commentary/corporations-are-finally-giving-dei-the-pink-slip.

6. *In announcing a shift*: Edward Helmore, "Harley-Davidson drops DEI initiatives amid pressure from 'anti-woke' activists," *The Guardian*, August 20, 2024, https://www.theguardian.com/us-news/article/2024/aug/20/harley-davidson-drops-diversity-initiatives.

6. *Boeing stated*: Kristen Parisi, "Boeing dissolves its DE&I team, amid ongoing problems for the aircraft company," *HR Brew*, November 1, 2024, https://www.hr-brew.com/stories/2024/11/01/boeing-dissolves-its-de-and-i-team-amid-ongoing-problems-for-the-aircraft-company.

6. *Lowe's proclaimed*: Robby Starbuck (@robbystarbuck), X, August 26, 2024, https://x.com/robbystarbuck/status/1828124701689876947.

6. *The education sector*: "University DEI: Status Quo and Rebrands," Defending Education, April 16, 2025, https://defendinged.org/investigations/university-dei-offices-and-programming/.

7. *More than half of Americans*: William H. Frey, "New 2020 census results show increased diversity countering decade-long declines in America's white and youth populations," Brookings, August 13, 2021, https://www.brookings.edu/articles/new-2020-census-results-show-increased-diversity-countering-decade-long-declines-in-americas-white-and-youth-populations/; William H. Frey, "The US will become 'minority white' in 2045, Census projects," Brookings, March 14, 2018, https://www.brookings.edu/articles/the-us-will-become-minority-white-in-2045-census-projects/.

7. *More than a quarter*: Matt Lavietes, "Nearly 30% of Gen Z adults identify as LGBTQ, national survey finds," NBC News, January 24, 2024, https://www.nbcnews.com/nbc-out/out-news/nearly-30-gen-z-adults-identify-lgbtq-national-survey-finds-rcna135510.

7. *Women outnumber men*: Richard Fry, "Women now outnumber men in

the U.S. college-educated labor force," Pew Research Center, September 26, 2022, https://www.pewresearch.org/short-reads/2022/09/26/women-now-outnumber-men-in-the-u-s-college-educated-labor-force/.

8. *To survive, this project*: Some of the ideas in this book, including this use of the irresistible force paradox, were first introduced in our article "The Irresistible Force and the Immovable Object: *Students for Fair Admissions* and Workplace DEI," *American Journal of Law and Equality* 4 (2024): 178–200, https://doi.org/10.1162/ajle_a_00067.

9. *We maintain a public educational tracker*: Advancing DEI Initiative (website), accessed August 28, 2025, https://advancingdei.meltzercenter.org/.

12. *There's an old labor activist*: "Quote wrongly attributed to Mahatma Gandhi," Associated Press, October 5, 2018, https://apnews.com/article/archive-fact-checking-2315880316.

12. *After President Barack Obama's*: Dr. James J. Zogby, "Demographics Aren't Destiny," *The Nation*, June 2, 2024, https://www.nation.com.pk/02-Jun-2024/demographics-aren-t-destiny; Anthony Zurcher, "Democrats' bet on a generation of liberal voters has backfired badly," BBC, November 9, 2024, https://www.bbc.com/news/articles/c0mzl7zygpmo.

13. *Even though his agenda*: Hannah Hartig, "2. Voting patterns in the 2024 election," Pew Research Center, June 26, 2025, https://www.pewresearch.org/politics/2025/06/26/voting-patterns-in-the-2024-election/.

STRATEGY 1: REVEAL THE STAKES

15. *He called Mexican immigrants*: Stephen Piggott, "Hate in the Race," Southern Poverty Law Center, July 6, 2016, https://www.splcenter.org/resources/reports/hate-race/; "Trump has long history of offensive comments about women," PBS, October 9, 2016, https://www.pbs.org/newshour/politics/trump-offensive-comments-women.

16. *In her 2022 book*: Joanna Williams, *How Woke Won: The Elitist Movement That Threatens Democracy, Tolerance and Reason* (Wanstead, UK: John Wilkes Publishing, 2022), 1.

16. *Right-wing author*: Richard Hanania, *The Origins of Woke: Civil Rights Law, Corporate America, and the Triumph of Identity Politics* (New York: HarperCollins Publishers, 2023), x.
16. *The dominance of the DEI agenda*: Christopher F. Rufo, *America's Cultural Revolution: How the Radical Left Conquered Everything* (New York: Broadside Books, 2023).
16. *As politician Pete Buttigieg*: "1 Politician vs 25 Undecided Voters (Feat. Pete Buttigieg) | Surrounded," Jubilee, YouTube video, November 3, 2024, 34:28, https://www.youtube.com/watch?v=YE1f3n_n9UA.
16. *Opponents flipped this script*: Kristen Parisi, "Senate Judiciary Committee holds hearing focusing largely on DEI rebrands," *HR Brew*, July 28, 2025, https://www.hr-brew.com/stories/2025/07/28/senate-judiciary-committee-holds-hearing-on-dei-focusing-largely-on-dei-rebrands.
16. *They framed DEI supporters*: See, e.g., Mike Gonzalez, "How Trump Is Uprooting Radical '60s Foundations of Poisonous DEI and CRT Programs," The Heritage Foundation, February 11, 2025, https://www.heritage.org/progressivism/commentary/how-trump-uprooting-radical-60s-foundations-poisonous-dei-and-crt-programs; Christopher F. Rufo, "What critical race theory is really about," *New York Post*, May 6, 2021, https://nypost.com/2021/05/06/what-critical-race-theory-is-really-about/; Erec Smith, "Sacrificing Excellence for Ideology: The Real Cost of DEI," Cato Institute, June 25, 2025, https://www.cato.org/testimony/sacrificing-excellence-ideology-real-cost-dei.
16. *They highlighted the most*: Kirsten Fleming, "Matt Walsh exposes antiracist 'grifters' getting rich off white guilt: 'Selling a disease without a cure,'" *New York Post*, September 9, 2024, https://nypost.com/2024/09/09/opinion/matt-walsh-exposes-the-gurus-getting-rich-off-white-guilt/.
17. *While slamming the idea*: "Unequal Protection: The Push to Replace 'Equality' with 'Equity' Is Unconstitutional," The Heritage Foundation, YouTube video, September 23, 2021, 0:30, https://www.youtube.com/watch?v=YLTiMu11zz8&t=3s.

17. *Legal strategist Edward Blum*: Freddie Sayers, "Edward Blum: My battle against affirmative action: Meet the strategist who campaigned for today's Supreme Court decision," *Unherd*, June 29, 2023, https://unherd.com/2023/06/edward-blum-my-battle-against-affirmative-action-2/.

17. *Utah governor Spencer Cox*: Jonathon Sharp, "Gov. Cox pens 5,000-word essay on why he signed DEI bill," ABC4, February 19, 2024, https://www.abc4.com/news/politics/gov-cox-pens-5000-word-essay-on-why-he-signed-dei-bill/.

17. *And Christopher Rufo called*: Christopher F. Rufo, "A New Civil Rights Agenda," *City Journal*, January 17, 2024, https://www.city-journal.org/article/a-new-civil-rights-agenda.

18. *The* New York Times *gave*: Nicholas Confessore, "'America Is Under Attack': Inside the Anti-D.E.I. Crusade," *New York Times*, January 20, 2024, https://www.nytimes.com/interactive/2024/01/20/us/dei-woke-claremont-institute.html.

18. *Wax was under investigation*: Vimal Patel, "UPenn Accuses a Law Professor of Racist Statements. Should She Be Fired?," *New York Times*, March 13, 2023, https://www.nytimes.com/2023/03/13/us/upenn-law-professor-racism-freedom-speech.html.

19. *She has argued publicly*: Ibid; Isaac Chotiner, "A Penn Law Professor Wants to Make America White Again," *The New Yorker*, August 23, 2019, https://www.newyorker.com/news/q-and-a/a-penn-law-professor-wants-to-make-america-white-again.

19. *Trump State Department appointee*: Aishvarya Kavi, "Fired Speechwriter from First Trump Term Appointed to Lead the Institute of Peace," *New York Times*, July 25, 2025, https://www.nytimes.com/2025/07/25/admin/darren-beattie-institute-of-peace.html.

19. *Laura Loomer, a right-wing*: Shaniqua McClendon, "Opinion: Laura Loomer knew what she was doing when she called Kamala Harris 'Shaniqua,'" *USA Today*, September 26, 2024, https://www.usatoday.com/story/opinion/voices/2024/09/26/trump-laura-loomer-racist-tropes-black-women-dei/75313176007/.

19. *Political commentator and DEI opponent*: Madeline Peltz, "Career women in right-wing media tell young girls to give up their dreams at Young Women's Leadership Summit," *Media Matters*, June 11, 2023, https://www.mediamatters.org/charlie-kirk/career-women-right-wing-media-tell-young-girls-give-their-dreams-young-womens; Rachel Dobkin, "Candace Owens Is 'Terrified' of Women Pilots," *Newsweek*, January 26, 2024, https://www.newsweek.com/candace-owens-terrified-women-pilots-1864495; Turning Point USA (@turningpointusa), "Candace CRUSHES the Left's DEI Identity," YouTube video, April 29, 2024, https://www.youtube.com/shorts/Sns7pamkY54.

19. *Conservative podcast host*: Matt Lamb, "Matt Walsh tells Tucker Carlson homosexual adoption is an 'abomination,'" LifeSiteNews, May 5, 2025, https://www.lifesitenews.com/news/matt-walsh-tells-tucker-carlson-homosexual-adoption-is-an-abomination/; IMDb, "Am I Racist?" accessed September 15, 2025, https://www.imdb.com/title/tt33034103/.

19. *And Secretary of Defense Pete Hegseth*: Pete Hegseth (@Pete Hegseth), "All of Christ for All of Life," X, August 7, 2025, https://x.com/PeteHegseth/status/1953626931234054558,

19. *Hegseth has also called for*: Pete Hegseth, *Battle for the American Mind: Uprooting a Century of Miseducation* (New York: Broadside Books, 2022), 231–37.

20. *Seventy-four percent of Fortune 50*: "The diversity of the top 50 Fortune 500 CEOs over time," Qualtrics, August 4, 2023, https://www.qualtrics.com/blog/fortune-500-ceo-diversity/.

20. *Four percent of such CEOs*: Eva Roytburg, "The number of Black Fortune 500 CEOs is still abysmally low. A 'shocking' corporate DEI practice might be to blame, Stanford professor says," *Fortune*, June 19, 2024, https://fortune.com/2024/06/19/the-number-of-black-fortune-500-ceos-is-still-abysmally-low-a-shocking-corporate-dei-practice-might-be-to-blame-stanford-professor-says/.

20. *Panning out a bit*: Richie Zweigenhaft, "White men are now less than half of corporate board members—after a decade of progress," *The*

Conversation, March 13, 2024, https://theconversation.com/white-men-are-now-less-than-half-of-corporate-board-members-after-a-decade-of-progress-224892; NALP, "2024 Report on Diversity in U.S. Law Firms," January 2025, https://www.nalp.org/uploads/Research/2024-25_NALPReportonDiversity.pdf; Katherine Schaeffer, "119th Congress brings new growth in racial, ethnic diversity to Capitol Hill," Pew Research Center, January 21, 2025, https://www.pewresearch.org/short-reads/2025/01/21/119th-congress-brings-new-growth-in-racial-ethnic-diversity-to-capitol-hill/; Anna Jackson, "Women account for 28% of lawmakers in the 119th Congress—unchanged from the last Congress," Pew Research Center, February 21, 2025, https://www.pewresearch.org/short-reads/2025/02/21/women-account-for-28-of-lawmakers-in-the-119th-congress-unchanged-from-the-last-congress/.

21. *In his 2024 book*: Charles Gasparino, *Go Woke, Go Broke: The Inside Story of the Radicalization of Corporate America* (New York: Center Street, 2024), 14.

21. *In an interview*: Lulu Garcia-Navarro, "He Worked for Years to Overturn Affirmative Action and Finally Won. He's Not Done," *New York Times*, July 8, 2023, https://www.nytimes.com/2023/07/08/us/edward-blum-affirmative-action-race.html.

21. *Here's author Coleman Hughes*: Coleman Hughes, *The End of Race Politics: Arguments for a Colorblind America* (New York: Thesis, 2024), 115.

22. *Rufo also cites*: Ross Douthat, "The Anti-D.E.I. Crusader Who Wants to Dismantle the Department of Education," *New York Times*, March 7, 2025, https://www.nytimes.com/2025/03/07/opinion/chris-rufo-trump-anti-dei-education.html.

22. *Sportswriter Reagan Griffin Jr.* : Reagan Griffin Jr., "As March Madness rolls on, so will the myths of Black athletic superiority," *The Guardian*, March 29, 2021, https://www.theguardian.com/sport/2021/mar/29/black-athletes-genetically-superior-myth-sports.

22. *They chose a trade*: Kerry Miller, "Greener Shades for Nail Salons," *Bloomberg*, March 5, 2007, https://www.bloomberg.com/news/articles

/2007-03-05/greener-shades-for-nail-salonsbusinessweek-business-news-stock-market-and-financial-advice?embedded-checkout=true.

22. *This initial influx*: Thanh Lieu, "Nail salons and Vietnamese refugees: Finding sanctuary in an unexpected place," National Museum of American History, February 29, 2024, https://americanhistory.si.edu/explore/stories/finding-sanctuary-unexpected-place.

23. *In a 2024 study*: SPR, "Women in Tech Statistics: 73% Experience Gender Bias in the Workplace," February 6, 2024, https://spr.com/women-in-tech-statistics/.

24. *As the Supreme Court observed*: Students for Fair Admissions, Inc. v. President & Fellows of Harvard Coll., 600 U.S. 181, 220 (2023).

24. *Conversely, if race is*: For more on "thick" and "thin" conceptions of race, see Reva B. Siegel, "The Racial Rhetorics of Colorblind Constitutionalism: The Case of Hopwood v. Texas," in *Race and Representation: Affirmative Action*, ed. Robert Post and Michael Rogin (New York: Zone Books, 1998), 29.

25. *In the Supreme Court's 2023*: Students for Fair Admissions, Inc., 206.

25. *If we look at the*: Regents of the University of California v. Bakke, 438 U.S. 265 (1978); Fullilove v. Klutznick, 448 U.S. 448 (1980).

25. *We then see a shift*: Grutter v. Bollinger, 539 U.S. 306 (2003); Fisher v. University of Texas, 570 U.S. 297 (2013).

26. *While the bill didn't*: Kate Sosin, "Trans youth sports debate consumes Equality Act Senate hearing," *19th News*, March 18, 2021, https:/19thnews.org/2021/03/trans-youth-sports-debate-consumes-equality-act-senate-hearing/.

26. *After listening to*: Hearings on H.R. 5, The Equality Act, First Session, before the Comm. on the Judiciary, 116th Cong. (2019) (statements of Rep. Ted Deutch and Rep. Louis Gohmert).

26. *Gohmert notably*: Ibid.

26. *Take Christopher Rufo*: Christopher Rufo, "A New Civil Rights Agenda," *City Journal*, January 17, 2024, https://www.city-journal.org/article/a-new-civil-rights-agenda; Christopher F. Rufo, "D.E.I. Programs Are Getting in the Way of Liberal Education," *New York Times*,

July 27, 2023, https://www.nytimes.com/2023/07/27/opinion/christopher-rufo-diversity-desantis-florida-university.html.
26. *Formerly, about two-thirds*: Michelle Goldberg, "At a College Targeted by DeSantis, Gender Studies Is Out, Jocks Are In," *New York Times*, August 14, 2023, https://www.nytimes.com/2023/08/14/opinion/columnists/gender-studies-ron-desantis-florida.html.
26. *Yet as journalist Michelle Goldberg*: Ibid.
27. *Rufo approvingly observes*: Ibid.
27. *Richard Hanania, whose ideas*: Noel King and Miles Bryan, "The man whose tweets helped kill DEI," *Vox*, March 15, 2025, https://www.vox.com/today-explained-podcast/404120/richard-hanania-dei-policy-trump; Richard Hanania, *The Origins of Woke: Civil Rights Law, Corporate America, and the Triumph of Identity Politics* (New York: HarperCollins Publishers, 2023), 202–3.
28. *Influential conservative journalist*: Christopher Caldwell, *The Age of Entitlement: America Since the Sixties* (New York: Simon & Schuster Paperbacks, 2020), 278.

STRATEGY 2: SUPPORT DISSENT

30. *Journalist Brock Colyar*: Brock Colyar, "The Cruel Kids' Table," *New York Magazine*, January 27, 2025, https://nymag.com/intelligencer/article/inauguration-trump-supporters-conservative-movement-post-maga.html.
30. *Like Colyar*: Shadi Hamid, "The beginning of the end of the Trump era," *Washington Post*, March 27, 2025, https://www.washingtonpost.com/opinions/2025/03/27/trump-democrats-power-shift/.
30. *To draw on a colorful scenario*: David Sedaris, "Undecided," *The New Yorker*, October 20, 2008, https://www.newyorker.com/magazine/2008/10/27/undecided.
31. *Although we hear*: Ben Shapiro, "'Diversity Equity & Inclusion' Really Means Shut Up," speech recording, posted August 24, 2022, YouTube, 9 min., 41 sec., 2:33, https://www.youtube.com/watch?v=OZtlBuHNzaQ.

31. *Her blockbuster book*: "Paperback Nonfiction," *New York Times*, January 31, 2021, https://www.nytimes.com/books/best-sellers/2021/01/31/paperback-nonfiction/.
31. *Given the influence*: Robin DiAngelo, *White Fragility: Why It's So Hard for White People to Talk About Racism* (Boston: Beacon Press, 2018), 119.
32. *But as former Georgia House*: Rebecca Traister, "Stacey Abrams on Finishing the Job in Georgia," *The Cut*, November 19, 2020, https://www.thecut.com/2020/11/stacey-abrams-on-flipping-georgia-blue.html.
32. *It leads to what*: Timur Kuran, *Private Truths, Public Lies: The Social Consequences of Preference Falsification* (Cambridge, Massachusetts: Harvard University Press, 1997).
33. *Natalie Wynn, a political commentator*: "Transcript: Ezra Klein Interviews Natalie Wynn and Will Wilkinson," *New York Times*, April 27, 2021, https://www.nytimes.com/2021/04/27/podcasts/ezra-klein-podcast-cancel-culture-transcript.html.
34. *As columnist Michelle Goldberg*: "Transcript: Ezra Klein Interviews Michelle Goldberg," *New York Times*, July 8, 2022, https://www.nytimes.com/2022/07/08/podcasts/transcript-ezra-klein-interviews-michelle-goldberg.html.
34. *Journalist Anand Giridharadas*: Anand Giridharadas, *The Persuaders: At the Front Lines of the Fight for Hearts, Minds, and Democracy* (New York: Alfred A. Knopf, 2022), 13.
34. *Consider the findings*: "The Hidden Tribes of America" (website), accessed August 18, 2025, https://hiddentribes.us/.
35. *And in case you're wondering*: Kristen Soltis Anderson, "Politicians Are Polarized. American Voters, Not So Much," *New York Times*, August 29, 2025, https://www.nytimes.com/2025/08/29/opinion/american-politics-center.html.
35. *Representative Sarah McBride*: Hanna Rosin, "Democrats Need 'Imperfect Allies,'" *The Atlantic*, April 17, 2025, https://www.theatlantic.com/podcasts/archive/2025/04/sarah-mcbride-is-used-to-the-hate/682368/.

36. *In a conversation with*: Tema Okun, "White Supremacy Culture," accessed August 18, 2025, https://cdn.ymaws.com/www.wpha.org/resource/resmgr/health_&_racial_equity/whitesupremacycultureinorgan.pdf.
36. *Yet it spread like wildfire*: Maurice Mitchell, "Building Resilient Organizations," *The Forge*, November 29, 2022, https://forgeorganizing.org/article/building-resilient-organizations/; "Tema Okun on Her Mythical Paper on White Supremacy," *The Intercept*, February 3, 2023, https://theintercept.com/2023/02/03/deconstructed-tema-okun-white-supremacy/.
36. *Engineering professor*: Chris Cooper, "A Call for Moderate Voices on DEI," *Inside Higher Ed*, June 12, 2025, https://www.insidehighered.com/opinion/views/2025/06/12/call-moderate-voices-dei-opinion.
37 *Our previous book was devoted*: Kenji Yoshino and David Glasgow, *Say the Right Thing: How to Talk About Identity, Diversity, and Justice* (New York: Atria, 2023).
37. *Consider the widely pilloried*: "Elimination of Harmful Language Initiative," Stanford University (2022), https://s.wsj.net/public/resources/documents/stanfordlanguage.pdf.
37. *Opponents of DEI are banning*: Tom Bowman, "U.S. Army libraries target books with a focus on DEI or 'gender ideology' for removal," NPR, April 15, 2025, https://www.npr.org/2025/04/15/nx-s1-5366122/army-libraries-books-dei-gender-ideology; Jeffrey Adam Sachs, "Steep Rise in Gag Orders, Many Sloppily Drafted," PEN America, January 24, 2022, https://pen.org/steep-rise-gag-orders-many-sloppily-drafted/; Cristina Portela Solomon and Kate L. Pamperin, "Florida's 'Stop Woke' Act Limits the Topics Employers Can Discuss in D&I Training," *National Law Review*, March 28, 2022, https://natlawreview.com/article/florida-s-stop-woke-act-limits-topics-employers-can-discuss-di-training; Aaron Blake, "Trump wants a federal protest crackdown—or, at least, the illusion of one," CNN, June 10, 2025, https://www.cnn.com/2025/06/10/politics/trump-la-protest-crackdown; Cecilia Kang, "Brendan Carr Plans to Keep Going After the Media," *New York Times*,

September 24, 2025, https://www.nytimes.com/2025/09/24/technology/brendan-carr-fcc-kimmel.html; Kathryn Watson, "Federal judge tosses Trump's lawsuit against New York Times, calls complaint 'decidedly improper and impermissible,'" CBS News, September 19, 2025, https://www.cbsnews.com/news/federal-judge-rejects-trump-lawsuit-new-york-times-reporters/; Karen Yourish et al., "These Words Are Disappearing in the New Trump Administration," *New York Times*, March 7, 2025, https://www.nytimes.com/interactive/2025/03/07/us/trump-federal-agencies-websites-words-dei.html.

38. *In 2022, the Florida*: H.R. 7, 124th Leg. Reg. Sess. (Fla. 2022).
38. *A federal court struck*: Honeyfund.com Inc. v. Governor, 94 F.4th 1272 (2024).
38. *The appeals court observed*: Ibid., 1275.
38. *Free speech arguments*: Jessica Guynn, "Donald Trump executive order banning diversity training blocked by federal judge," *USA Today*, December 23, 2020, https://www.usatoday.com/story/money/2020/12/23/trump-diversity-training-ban-executive-order-blocked-federal-judge/4033590001/.
38. *Presumably, the administration realized*: Exec. Order No. 14173, 90 Fed. Reg. 8633 (January 31, 2025). ("This order does not prevent State or local governments, Federal contractors, or Federally-funded [sic] State and local educational agencies or institutions of higher education from engaging in First Amendment-protected speech.")
38. *And while the conservative*: See, e.g., 303 Creative LLC v. Elenis, 600 U.S. 570 (2023); Janus v. AFSCME, 585 U.S. 878 (2018).
39. *We agree with human rights advocate*: Suzanne Nossel, *Dare to Speak: Defending Free Speech for All* (New York: Dey Street, 2020), 4.
39. *As Nossel points out*: Ibid., 14.
39. *Finally, look for*: Jonah Berger, *The Catalyst: How to Change Anyone's Mind* (New York: Simon & Schuster Paperbacks, 2020), 97.
41. *If everyone who makes*: Some of our ideas in this section were first set out in our op-ed: Kenji Yoshino and David Glasgow, "Cancel culture has its merits, but the left is ready for a better approach," *Los*

Angeles Times, March 17, 2023, https://www.latimes.com/opinion/story/2023-03-17/cancel-culture-racism-sexism-bias.

41. *As psychologist Scott Plous observes*: S. Plous, "Responding to Overt Displays of Prejudice: A Role-Playing Exercise," *Teaching of Psychology* 27, no. 3 (August 2000): 198–200, https://doi.org/10.1207/S15328023TOP2703_07.

42. *Yet the irony*: Loretta J. Ross, *Calling In: How to Start Making Change with Those You'd Rather Cancel* (New York: Simon & Schuster, 2025), 70.

STRATEGY 3: WELCOME NEW GROUPS

47. *Nevertheless, decades later*: Caroline Casey, "Do Your D&I Efforts Include People with Disabilities?," *Harvard Business Review*, March 19, 2020, https://hbr.org/2020/03/do-your-di-efforts-include-people-with-disabilities.

47. *Congress enacted age discrimination*: Scott Birch, "Ageism in the workplace—the forgotten DE&I factor," *Sustainability Magazine*, October 18, 2022, https://sustainabilitymag.com/diversity-and-inclusion-dandi/ageism-in-the-workplace-the-forgotten-de-i-factor.

47. *People of faith have repeatedly*: West Virginia State Board of Education v. Barnette, 319 U.S. 624 (1943); Wisconsin v. Yoder, 406 U.S. 205 (1972); Groff v. DeJoy, 600 U.S. 447 (2023); Sherbert v. Verner, 374 U.S. 398 (1963).

47. *Eboo Patel, the founder*: "How to Build a Diverse Democracy," November 12, 2024, posted November 26, 2024, by NYU School of Law, YouTube, 36:25, https://www.youtube.com/watch?v=PkB30cWQtlw&t=2232s.

47. *Patel's colleague, Megan Johnson*: Jennifer Miller, "What Happens When the Boss Invites You to Bible Study?," *New York Times*, September 22, 2023, https://www.nytimes.com/2023/09/22/business/religion-work-diversity-equity-inclusion.html.

47. *In our experience*: Dawit Habtemariam, "How to Become a Chief Diversity Officer," *Senior Executive*, April 7, 2022, https://senior

executive.com/how-to-become-a-chief-diversity-officer/; "In America, Does More Education Equal Less Religion?," Pew Research Center, April 26, 2017, https://www.pewresearch.org/religion/2017/04/26/in-america-does-more-education-equal-less-religion/.

47. *They're also less likely*: "In America, Does More Education Equal Less Religion?," Pew Research Center, April 26, 2017, https://www.pewresearch.org/religion/2017/04/26/in-america-does-more-education-equal-less-religion/.

47. *Yet it's self-destructive*: "How Religious Are Americans?," Gallup, March 29, 2024, https://news.gallup.com/poll/358364/religious-americans.aspx.

47. *The United States has a high*: Dalia Fahmy, "Americans are far more religious than adults in other wealthy nations," Pew Research Center, July 31, 2018, https://www.pewresearch.org/short-reads/2018/07/31/americans-are-far-more-religious-than-adults-in-other-wealthy-nations/.

48. *Muslim scholar Nadia Ahmad*: Nadia Ahmad, "How DEI Initiatives on Islamophobia Fall Short," *Inside Higher Ed*, October 18, 2024, https://www.insidehighered.com/opinion/career-advice/conditionally-accepted/2024/10/18/how-dei-initiatives-islamophobia-fall-short.

48. *Evelyn Alsultany*: Evelyn Alsultany, "Diversity Initiatives Are Failing the U.S. Muslim Community," *Time*, November 28, 2022, https://time.com/6235828/diversity-initiatives-failing-us-muslim-community/; Anne Barnard, "Painful memory for Muslims: Outrage over a proposed Islamic center in Manhattan," *New York Times*, September 11, 2021, https://www.nytimes.com/2021/09/11/nyregion/muslim-islamic-center-9-11.html.

48. *Whether Jewish identity*: "Jewish identity and belief," Pew Research Center, May 11, 2021, https://www.pewresearch.org/religion/2021/05/11/jewish-identity-and-belief/.

48. *A Jewish person faces*: "Antisemitism Is an Urgent Problem. Too Many People Are Making Excuses," *New York Times*, June 14, 2025, https://www.nytimes.com/2025/06/14/opinion/antisemitism-jewish-hate.html.

48. *Antisemitic hate speech*: "Understanding Antisemitism on Social Media," Center for Countering Digital Hate, February 23, 2024, https://counterhate.com/blog/understanding-antisemitism-on-social-media/.

48. *Synagogues are being vandalized*: David Ibave, "2 El Paso synagogues vandalized with Nazi symbols, investigated as potential hate crime," KFox14, February 6, 2025, https://kfoxtv.com/news/local/el-paso-synagogue-vandalized-with-nazi-symbols-investigated-as-potential-hate-crime-texas-tx-cherry-hill-lane-bnai-zion-congregation-synagogue-fbi-graffiti.

48. *In a 2024 survey*: American Jewish Committee, "The State of Antisemitism in America 2024," https://www.ajc.org/AntisemitismReport2024.

48. *Yet Jewish DEI advocate*: Debbie Epstein Henry, "Why Jews Belong Under the Diversity, Equity, and Inclusion Umbrella," *The American Lawyer*, December 19, 2023, https://www.law.com/americanlawyer/2023/12/19/why-jews-belong-under-the-diversity-equity-and-inclusion-umbrella/.

49. *It's one thing to argue*: See, e.g., "Secretary McMahon Statement on Columbia University Deal," U.S. Department of Education, July 23, 2025, https://www.ed.gov/about/news/press-release/secretary-mcmahon-statement-columbia-university-deal.

49. *Even assuming the administration*: Laura Meckler et al., "Inside the powerful task force spearheading Trump's assault on colleges, DEI," *Washington Post*, July 24, 2025, https://www.washingtonpost.com/education/2025/07/18/antisemitism-task-force-dei-universities-trump/.

49. *In recent years*: Jennifer Miller, "What Happens When the Boss Invites You to Bible Study?," *New York Times*, September 22, 2023, https://www.nytimes.com/2023/09/22/business/religion-work-diversity-equity-inclusion.html.

49. *Consider philosopher Paul Gottfried's*: Paul Gottfried, "America Is Not an 'Idea,'" *Chronicles*, March 16, 2021, https://chroniclesmagazine.org/web/america-is-not-an-idea/.

50. *To us, the most prominent*: Richard V. Reeves, *Of Boys and Men: Why the Modern Male Is Struggling, Why It Matters, and What to Do About It* (Washington, D.C.: Brookings Institution, 2022).
50. *In that work*: Ibid., x, xi, 30.
50. *Boys are more likely*: Ibid., x, 5, 7.
50. *Over the past few decades*: Ibid., 19–21.
50. *Men are also more likely*: Claire Cain Miller, "It's Not Just a Feeling: Data Shows Boys and Young Men Are Falling Behind," *New York Times*, May 13, 2025, https://www.nytimes.com/2025/05/13/upshot/boys-falling-behind-data.html?smid=nytcore-ios-share&referringSource=articleShare; Beth Connolly, "Men More Likely Than Women to Face Substance Use Disorders and Mental Illness," Pew, June 3, 2019, https://www.pew.org/en/research-and-analysis/articles/2019/06/03/men-more-likely-than-women-to-face-substance-use-disorders-and-mental-illness; Ravan Hawrami, Noah Hendelman, and Alanna Williams, "Male homelessness in the United States," *American Institute for Boys and Men*, February 27, 2025, https://aibm.org/research/homelessness-in-the-united-states/; Helene Schumacher, "Why more men than women die by suicide," BBC, March 17, 2019, https://www.bbc.com/future/article/20190313-why-more-men-kill-themselves-than-women.
50. *Reeves doesn't argue*: Reeves, *Of Boys and Men*, ix–x, 115.
50. *Nor could he*: Gabrielle Ulubay and Brooke Knappenberger, "36 Ways Women Still Aren't Equal to Men," *Marie Claire*, March 8, 2023, https://www.marieclaire.com/politics/news/a15652/gender-inequality-stats/.
50. *Instead, he argues*: Reeves, *Of Boys and Men*, 115.
50. *Societies, he contends*: Ibid., 150–66.
51. *In an educational setting*: Zara Abrams, "Boys are facing key challenges in school. Inside the effort to support their success," American Psychological Association, April 1, 2023, https://www.apa.org/monitor/2023/04/boys-school-challenges-recommendations; Elizabeth Heubeck and Francis Sheehan, "Teachers, Here's How to Build Stronger Relationships With Boys (Downloadable)," *Education Week*, January 27, 2025,

https://www.edweek.org/teaching-learning/teachers-heres-how-to-build-stronger-relationships-with-boys-downloadable/2025/01.

51. *One survey of frontline workers*: Sheila Brassel, *How to Reduce Gender-Based Hostility in Frontline Workplaces* (New York: Catalyst, 2024), https://www.catalyst.org/insights/2024/reduce-sexist-behavior-frontline-workplace.

52. *On any number of measures*: The statistics in this paragraph are drawn from Matt Grossman and David A. Hopkins, *Polarized by Degrees: How the Diploma Divide and the Culture War Transformed American Politics* (Cambridge, England: Cambridge University Press, 2024), 40; Jennifer C. Pan, *Selling Social Justice: Why the Rich Love Antiracism* (London: Verso, 2025), 85–89.

52. *As the American economy has shifted*: Emily Badger, Robert Gebeloff, and Aatish Bhatia, "They Used to Be Ahead in the American Economy. Now They've Fallen Behind," *New York Times*, October 26, 2024, https://www.nytimes.com/interactive/2024/10/26/upshot/census-relative-income.html,

52. *Parental income almost perfectly*: Thomas Piketty, *A Brief History of Equality* (Cambridge, Massachusetts: Harvard University Press, 2022), 176.

52. *Many elite colleges*: "Some Colleges Have More Students from the Top 1 Percent Than the Bottom 60. Find Yours," *New York Times*, January 18, 2017, https://www.nytimes.com/interactive/2017/01/18/upshot/some-colleges-have-more-students-from-the-top-1-percent-than-the-bottom-60.html. See also: Aatish Bhatia, Claire Cain Miller, and Josh Katz, "Study of Elite College Admissions Data Suggests Being Very Rich Is Its Own Qualification," *New York Times*, July 24, 2023, https://www.nytimes.com/interactive/2023/07/24/upshot/ivy-league-elite-college-admissions.html.

52. *People from lower socioeconomic*: Paul Ingram and Jean Joohyun Oh, "Mapping the Class Ceiling: The Social Class Disadvantage for Attaining Management Positions," *Academy of Management Discoveries* 8, no. 1 (March 2022), https://doi.org/10.5465/amd.2020.0030.

52. *For those who seek employment*: Lauren Rivera, *Pedigree: How Elite Students Get Elite Jobs* (Princeton: Princeton University Press, 2015).
53. *College graduates represent*: Jennifer E. Manning, *Membership of the 119th Congress: A Profile* (Washington, D.C.: Congressional Research Service, August 4, 2025), https://www.congress.gov/crs-product/R48535; "Census Bureau Releases New Educational Attainment Data," U.S. Census Bureau, February 16, 2023, https://www.census.gov/newsroom/press-releases/2023/educational-attainment-data.html.
53. *While less than 10 percent*: Dustin Guastella, "The wealthy dominate government. Democrats should work to change that," *Washington Post*, April 24, 2024, https://www.washingtonpost.com/opinions/2024/04/24/democrats-working-class-candidates-wealthy-government/; Seamus Webster, "One out of every 15 Americans is a millionaire, UBS says," *Fortune*, July 29, 2024, https://fortune.com/2024/07/29/us-millionaires-population-ubs-global-wealth-report-china-europe-americans/.
53. *All these dynamics*: See, e.g., Victor Davis Hanson, "Wealthy and Woke," *National Review*, April 8, 2021, https://www.nationalreview.com/2021/04/wealthy-and-woke/.
54. *Faiz Shakir*: Noam Scheiber, "As Trump Attacks D.E.I., Some on the Left Approve," *New York Times*, February 6, 2025, https://www.nytimes.com/2025/02/06/business/economy/trump-dei-democrats-left-unions.html.
54. *Jennifer C. Pan*: Ibid.
54. *Given that the "diploma divide"*: Grossman and Hopkins, *Polarized by Degrees*.
55. *Columnist Megan McArdle*: Megan McArdle, "Abandoning DEI won't fix academia's left-leaning problem," *Washington Post*, March 23, 2025, https://www.washingtonpost.com/opinions/2025/03/23/academia-conservative-liberal-diversity-statements/.
56. *An organization can't engage*: Anti-DEI activists don't universally approve of class-based affirmative action. See Ryan Teague Beckwith, "There's a solution to the fight over DEI. Some conservatives are taking

aim at it," MSNBC, July 19, 2025, https://www.msnbc.com/opinion/msnbc-opinion/johns-hopkins-stephen-miller-america-first-legal-dei-affirmative-actio-rcna219607. In addition, while we have encouraged expanding DEI programs to include boys and men, legal restrictions on gender-based affirmative action programs would also place limitations on affirmative action programs or other preferences aimed at boys and men.

56. *Consider the case of*: Coalition for TJ v. Fairfax County School Board, 601 U.S. ___ (2024).
56. *Only time will tell*: For more on the legality of race-neutral methods of advancing racial diversity, see Sonja Starr, "The Magnet School Wars and the Future of Colorblindness," *Stanford Law Review* 76 (January 2024): 161.
56. *The laws relating to age*: In General Dynamics Land Systems, Inc. v. Cline, 540 U.S. 581 (2004), the U.S. Supreme Court held that the Age Discrimination in Employment Act doesn't prevent an employer from discriminating in favor of the old over the young, but rather only in favor of the young over the old. Similarly, the Americans with Disabilities Act (ADA) only protects discrimination against a "qualified individual on the basis of disability." Section 12201(g) of the ADA explicitly states: "Nothing in this chapter shall provide the basis for a claim by an individual without a disability that the individual was subject to discrimination because of the individual's lack of disability." Americans with Disabilities Act of 1990, 42 U.S.C. § 12101 et seq. (1990).
57. *In one study*: Modupe Akinola et al., "Does Broadening the Term 'Diversity' Correlate with a Lowered Representation of Racial Minorities and Women in Organizations?," *Academy of Management Discoveries* 10, no. 4 (December 2024): 568–88, https://doi.org/10.5465/amd.2020.0058.
57. *The researchers found*: Ibid., 577.
57. *While careful not to*: Ibid.
58. *An openness to new claims*: Kenji Yoshino, "The New Equal Protection," *Harvard Law Review* 124, no. 3 (January 2011).

59. *Many young men*: "Who is Andrew Tate? The self-proclaimed misogynist influencer," BBC, February 27, 2025, https://www.bbc.com/news/uk-64125045; Emmeline Saunders, "Big Brother reject Andrew Tate claims women 'should take personal responsibility' for rape in vile Harvey Weinstein rant," *Mirror*, October 19, 2017, https://www.mirror.co.uk/3am/celebrity-news/big-brother-reject-andrew-tate-11369506.

59. *In our presentations*: Kenji Yoshino and Christie Smith, *Uncovering Talent: A New Model of Inclusion* (New York: Deloitte Development LLC, 2013), https://www.lcld.com/wp-content/uploads/2023/06/Uncovering_Talent_Deloitte.pdf.

60. *In the early 1900s*: Savannah Cox, "How Left-Handedness Came to Be Seen As Evil," *All That's Interesting*, August 12, 2016, https://allthatsinteresting.com/left-handedness-evil/2.

60. *The court started by*: Frontiero v. Richardson, 411 U.S. 677 (1973); Bowen v. Gilliard, 483 U.S. 587 (1987).

60. *Weren't there other signs*: See, e.g., Cass R. Sunstein, "The Anticaste Principle," *Michigan Law Review* 92, no. 8 (1994), 2429.

60. *Were women politically powerful*: See, e.g., Frontiero v. Richardson, 411 U.S. 677 (1973).

60. *In a 1985 case*: City of Cleburne v. Cleburne Living Center, Inc., 473 U.S. 432, 446 (1985).

60. *And both before and after*: Eisenstadt v. Baird, 405 U.S. 438 (1972); Romer v. Evans, 517 U.S. 620 (1996); United States Department of Agriculture v. Moreno, 413 U.S. 528 (1973).

STRATEGY 4: LEVEL THE PLAYING FIELD

63. *In 2024, Elon Musk*: Ben Shapiro, "DEI Is Illegal | The Search with Ben Shapiro," Facebook, video, https://www.facebook.com/reel/403739202069035.

63. *In 2025, White House*: Stephen Miller (@StephenM), "DEI is illegal race-based discrimination in violation of the federal Civil Rights Act. A judge cannot nullify the Civil Rights Acts and order the

government to award federal taxpayer dollars to organizations that discriminate based on race," X, February 21, 2025, https://x.com/StephenM/status/1893111055007580410; "America First Legal Puts Woke Corporations, Law Firms, Hospitals on Notice: All DEI Programs and Workplace 'Balancing' Based on Race, National Origin, and Sex Violate the Law," America First Legal, June 29, 2023, https://aflegal.org/press-release/america-first-legal-puts-woke-corporations-law-firms-and-hospitals-on-notice-all-dei-programs-and-workplace-balancing-based-on-race-national-origin-and-sex-violate-the-law/.

63. *The federal agency*: Ryan Golden, "4 big law firms agree not to label lawful programs as DEI, EEOC says," *HR Dive*, April 14, 2025, https://www.hrdive.com/news/four-big-law-firms-curb-dei-eeoc-settlements/745314/.

64. *By 2016, that number*: Iris Bohnet, *What Works: Gender Equality by Design* (Cambridge, Massachusetts: Harvard University Press, 2016), 1–2.

65. *Ryan Williams*: Nicquel Terry Ellis, "What is DEI, and why is it dividing America?," CNN, January 23, 2025, https://www.cnn.com/2025/01/22/us/dei-diversity-equity-inclusion-explained/index.html.

65. *Heather Mac Donald*: Heather Mac Donald, "Merit Over Identity," *City Journal*, April 11, 2023, https://www.city-journal.org/article/higher-ed-must-choose-merit-over-identity.

65. *This strategy is what*: Saleem Reshamwala, "High Heels, Violins, and a Warning," *New York Times*, December 16, 2016, https://www.nytimes.com/video/us/100000004818679/high-heels-violins-and-a-warning.html.

65. *Researchers argue*: Claudia Goldin and Cecilia Rouse, "Orchestrating Impartiality: The Impact of 'Blind' Auditions on Female Musicians," *American Economic Review* 90, no. 4 (2000): 715–41, 738, DOI:10.1257/aer.90.4.715.

66. *In Europe*: Bohnet, *What Works*, 131–32.

67. *There's a world of difference*: Neil Gotanda, "A Critique of 'Our Constitution Is Color-Blind,'" *Stanford Law Review* 44, no. 1 (1991): 18.

67. *Often, that project*: Jessica Hamilton Young, "Best Stephen Colbert Quotes," *Chron*, September 8, 2015, https://www.chron.com/culture/tv/slideshow/Best-Stephen-Colbert-Quotes-116551.php.
67. *Or: "I don't see race"* : Gabriel Arana, "Shades of Difference," *The American Prospect*, December 7, 2010, https://prospect.org/article/shades-difference/.
67. *As Coleman Hughes says*: Coleman Hughes, *The End of Race Politics: Arguments for a Colorblind America* (New York: Thesis, 2024), 19.
67. *An investment banker described*: Lauren Rivera, *Pedigree: How Elite Students Get Elite Jobs* (Princeton: Princeton University Press, 2015), 140.
68. *Rivera's study of entry-level*: Ibid., 145.
68. *Such a system*: Bohnet, *What Works*, 123–45.
69. *Correll also offered prescriptions*: Shelley J. Correll et al., "Inside the Black Box of Organizational Life: The Gendered Language of Performance Assessment," *American Sociological Review* 85 no. 6 (2020): 1022–1050, https://doi.org/10.1177/0003122420962080.
69. *When she spoke to us*: Kenji Yoshino and David Glasgow, "Steer Clear of 'Illegal DEI' with Leveling—Not Lifting—Programs," *Bloomberg*, February 10, 2025, https://news.bloomberglaw.com/us-law-week/steer-clear-of-illegal-dei-with-leveling-not-lifting-programs.
69. *Williams encourages organizations*: Equality Action Center and The Conference Board, *Traditional Bias Training Doesn't Work—Bias Interrupters Do*, June 2024, https://biasinterrupters.org/wp-content/uploads/2024/06/Traditional-Bias-Training-Doesnt-Work-Bias-Interrupters-Do.pdf.
70. *When managers received training*: Ibid., 11–12.
70. *Other studies have examined*: Harriet R. Tenenbaum and Martin D. Ruck, "Are teachers' expectations different for racial minority than for European American students? A meta-analysis," *Journal of Educational Psychology* 99, no. 2 (May 2007): 253–73, https://doi.org/10.1037/0022-0663.99.2.253; Brian Heseung Kim et al., "Letters of Recommendation by High School Counselors in Selective College

Admissions: Differences by Race and Socioeconomic Status in Letter Length and Topics Discussed," *Research in Higher Education* 66, no. 30 (July 2025), https://doi.org/10.1007/s11162-025-09847-5.

70. *One study found*: Lauren A. Rivera and András Tilcsik, "Scaling Down Inequality: Rating Scales, Gender Bias, and the Architecture of Evaluation," *American Sociological Review* 84, no. 2 (2019): 248–74, https://doi.org/10.1177/0003122419833360.

70. *a six-point scale*: Ibid., 267.

70. *They note various factors*: Ibid., 268.

71. *Sociologists Frank Dobbin*: Frank Dobbin and Alexandra Kalev, *Getting to Diversity: What Works and What Doesn't* (Cambridge, Massachusetts: The Belknap Press of Harvard University Press, 2022), 89.

71. *Their research has found*: Ibid., 92–93.

72. *A 2024 Manhattan Institute*: Jesse Arm, "America's New Consensus: A National Survey Analysis of the Political and Policy Preferences of Likely 2024 Voters," Manhattan Institute, July 16, 2024, https://manhattan.institute/article/americas-new-consensus.

72. *A 2024 national Bellwether Research*: Bellwether Research, *August 2024 Quantitative Research Report*, July 2024, https://www.resourceimpactdc.org/copy-of-june-2024-qualitative-research, 5.

72. *They underscored how*: Ibid., 26.

73. *Move toward statements like this*: The first part of this statement—"Talent is everywhere but opportunity is not"—is a common phrase in the DEI community of unclear origin.

73. *The unpopularity of lifting*: Justin McCarthy, "Post-Affirmative Action, Views on Admissions Differ by Race," Gallup, January 16, 2024, https://news.gallup.com/poll/548528/post-affirmative-action-views-admissions-differ-race.aspx; Michael Powell and Ilana Marcus, "The Failed Affirmative Action Campaign That Shook Democrats," *New York Times*, June 11, 2023, https://www.nytimes.com/2023/06/11/us/supreme-court-affirmative-action.html.

74. *Anthony Tommasini*: Anthony Tommasini, "To Make Orchestras More Diverse, End Blind Auditions," *New York Times*, July 16, 2020,

https://www.nytimes.com/2020/07/16/arts/music/blind-auditions-orchestras-race.html.

74. *In a 2025 Axios poll* :Emily Peck, "Americans are fine with corporate DEI," *Axios*, January 17, 2025, https://www.axios.com/2025/01/17/diversity-initiatives-workers-trump.

74. *A plurality of respondents*: AP-NORC Center for Public Affairs Research, "The public is skeptical about the effectiveness of DEI initiatives," July 31, 2025, https://apnorc.org/projects/the-public-is-skeptical-about-the-effectiveness-of-dei-initiatives/.

75. *Dobbin and Kalev*: Frank Dobbin and Alexandra Kalev, "Achieve DEI Goals Without DEI Programs," *Harvard Business Review*, July–August 2025, https://hbr.org/2025/07/achieve-dei-goals-without-dei-programs.

75. *Even Andrea Lucas*: Andrea Lucas, "DEI Perspectives from EEOC Commissioner Andrea Lucas," *Employment Law Now*, March 1, 2024, podcast, 34:11, https://www.employmentlawnow.com/2024/03/01/viii-141-dei-perspectives-from-eeoc-commissioner-andrea-lucas/.

76. *Andrea Lucas says*: Andrea Lucas (@andrealucasEEOC), "It's long past time for employers to ditch DEI & return to EEO [equal employment opportunity] & merit," X, January 6, 2025, https://x.com/andrealucasEEOC/status/1876442639282893159.

76. *The Trump administration's foremost*: Exec. Order No. 14173, 90 Fed. Reg. 8633 (January 31, 2025).

76. *And let's not forget*: Students for Fair Admissions, Inc. v. President & Fellows of Harvard Coll., 600 U.S. 181, 220, 206 (2023).

STRATEGY 5: EMBRACE THE UNIVERSAL

79. *On this occasion*: Haleluya Hadero, "Fund sued over grant program for Black women enlists prominent civil rights attorneys to fight back," Associated Press, August 10, 2023, https://apnews.com/article/edward-blum-fearless-fund-crump-affirmative-action-f4215ae5ccfbb8cebb56e280851e3ad2.

79. *The contest aimed*: Analisa Novak, "Fearless Fund CEO Arian Simone

on why she sees legal settlement as a win and what's next," CBS News, September 13, 2024, https://www.cbsnews.com/news/fearless-fund-arian-simone-legal-settlement/.
79. *Blum argued the program*: Jonathan Franklin, "A venture capital grant program for Black women officially ends after court ruling," NPR, September 11, 2024, https://www.npr.org/2024/09/11/nx-s1-5108729/fearless-fund-atlanta-grant-program-shut-down-lawsuit.
79. *This law was enacted*: Practical Law the Journal, "Origins of Section 1981 and Title VII," Reuters, February 2025, https://www.reuters.com/practical-law-the-journal/litigation/origins-section-1981-title-vii-2025-02-03/.
79. *On the heels of*: Tatyana Monnay, "Blum Says He's Done Suing Law Firms as Winston Yields on DEI," *Bloomberg*, December 6, 2023, https://news.bloomberglaw.com/business-and-practice/blum-says-hes-done-suing-law-firms-as-winston-yields-on-dei.
79. *McDonald's was sued*: Nate Raymond, "McDonald's sued over Latino scholarships despite rolling back diversity initiatives," Reuters, January 13, 2025, https://www.reuters.com/legal/mcdonalds-sued-over-latino-scholarships-despite-rolling-back-diversity-2025-01-13/.
80. *Hidden Star, a nonprofit*: Ann O'Leary and Marcus A.R. Childress, "Anti-DEI advocacy groups have a new target: minority-focused grant programs," *Daily Journal*, February 26, 2024, https://www.dailyjournal.com/articles/377324-anti-dei-advocacy-groups-have-a-new-target-minority-focused-grant-programs.
80. *The National Museum*: Suzanne Gamboa, "Smithsonian Latino museum internship is targeted by conservative legal activist," NBC News, February 23, 2024, https://www.nbcnews.com/news/latino/smithsonian-latino-museum-internship-targeted-conservative-legal-rcna140244.
80. *Lawsuits challenging targeted programs*: Advancing DEI Initiative Targeted Programs Cases (website), accessed August 20, 2025, https://advancingdei.meltzercenter.org/cases/?topic=targetedPrograms.
80. *The Fearless Fund seems to agree*: Alexandra Olson, "Fearless Fund

drops grant program for Black women business owners in lawsuit settlement," *Associated Press*, September 11, 2024, https://apnews.com/article/fearless-fund-dei-lawsuit-ed-blum-227a457ded5460061b4300a7ad16d18a.

81. *But as one wag*: German Lopez, "Why You Should Stop Saying 'All Lives Matter,' Explained in 9 Different Ways," *Vox*, July 11, 2016, https://www.vox.com/2016/7/11/12136140/black-all-lives-matter.

82. *This 1993 policy*: "Key Dates in U.S. Military LGBT Policy," U.S. Naval Institute, https://www.usni.org/naval-history-blog-collection/key-dates-u-s-military-lgbt-policy.

82. *This was done*: Sarah Pruitt, "Once Banned, Then Silenced: How Clinton's 'Don't Ask, Don't Tell' Policy Affected LGBTQ Military," History.com, April 25, 2018, https://www.history.com/articles/dont-ask-dont-tell-repeal-compromise.

82. *Gay people were at least*: Brooke Sopelsa, "Hundreds get honorable discharges after Pentagon's 'don't ask, don't tell' review," NBC News, October 15, 2024, https://www.nbcnews.com/nbc-out/out-politics-and-policy/dont-ask-dont-tell-honorable-discharge-pentagon-review-rcna175579.

83. *The first executive order*: Exec. Order No. 14173, 90 Fed. Reg. 8633 (January 31, 2025).

84. *Barely three months later*: Exec. Order No. 14283, 90 Fed. Reg. 17543 (April 28, 2025).

84. *It nevertheless required*: Taylor Telford, "Law firm opens diversity fellowship to all students after lawsuit," *Washington Post*, September 6, 2023, https://www.washingtonpost.com/business/2023/09/06/morrison-foerster-diversity-lawsuit-white-applicants/; Tatyana Monnay, "Morrison Foerster Changes DEI Fellowship Criteria Amid Lawsuit," *Bloomberg*, September 6, 2023, https://news.bloomberglaw.com/business-and-practice/morrison-foerster-changes-dei-fellowship-criteria-amid-lawsuit.

84. *After the firm*: Nate Raymond, "Affirmative action opponent drops case over Winston & Strawn's diversity fellowship," Reuters,

December 7, 2023, https://www.reuters.com/legal/legalindustry/affirmative-action-opponent-drops-case-over-winston-strawns-diversity-fellowship-2023-12-06/.

84. *McDonald's settled the lawsuit*: Samantha Elkins, "McDonald's to let white students apply for Latino scholarships after DEI lawsuit," *New York Post*, February 19, 2025, https://nypost.com/2025/02/19/business/mcdonalds-to-let-white-students-to-apply-for-latino-scholarships/.

85. *It too settled*: Jenny Brundin, "Scholarship won't just be for 'historically underrepresented' as CU med school settles lawsuit," *CPR News*, February 17, 2025, https://www.cpr.org/2025/02/17/scholarship-wont-just-be-for-historically-underrepresented-as-cu-med-school-settles-lawsuit/.

85. *Justice Ketanji Brown Jackson*: Students for Fair Admissions, Inc. v. University of North Carolina et al., No. 21-707, Oral Argument at 64–67, U.S. (October 31, 2022), https://www.supremecourt.gov/oral_arguments/argument_transcripts/2022/21-707_bb7j.pdf.

86. *After dismantling affirmative action*: Students for Fair Admissions, Inc. v. President & Fellows of Harvard Coll., 600 U.S. 181, 230 (2023).

86. *"The student must be treated"*: Ibid., 231.

86. *In our language*: In July 2025, Attorney General Pam Bondi released a memo that included "overcoming obstacles" narratives in a list of "potentially unlawful proxies." The memo is ambiguously worded, but doesn't appear to suggest that such narratives are inherently unlawful. Nor could it, given that the Supreme Court has clearly permitted them in some circumstances. See Pamela J. Bondi, Memorandum for All Federal Agencies (Washington, D.C.: U.S. Department of Justice, July 29, 2025), https://www.justice.gov/ag/media/1409486/dl.

86. *After it got sued*: Joint Stipulation of Dismissal at 1, Do No Harm v. Vituity, No 3:23-cv-24746 (N.D. Fla. 2023) (No. 23), https://donoharmmedicine.org/wp-content/uploads/2024/01/2024.01.02-Joint-Stipulation-of-Dismissal.pdf.

86. *The Small Business Administration*: Julian Mark, "He never saw himself

as disadvantaged. Then the government had him write an essay," *Washington Post*, June 29, 2024, https://www.washingtonpost.com/business/2024/06/29/sba-8a-curtis-joachim-racial-inequality/.

87. *In the educational realm*: Anemona Hartocollis and Colbi Edmonds, "Colleges Want to Know More About You and Your 'Identity,'" *New York Times*, August 14, 2023, https://www.nytimes.com/2023/08/14/us/college-applications-admissions-essay.html.

88. *As the Supreme Court has said*: Cummings v. Missouri, 71 U.S. 277, 325 (1867).

88. *After the Civil War*: Farrell Evans, "How Jim Crow–Era Laws Suppressed the African American Vote for Generations," History.com, May 13, 2021, https://www.history.com/articles/jim-crow-laws-black-vote.

88. *The ruling clearly prohibited*: Students for Fair Admissions, 230–31.

88. *In one unfortunate example*: Matt Vespa, "More Docs Show Belmont University Continuing Its DEI Shenanigans in Defiance of the Law," *Townhall*, July 30, 2025, https://townhall.com/tipsheet/mattvespa/2025/07/30/belmont-universitys-dei-shenanigans-are-still-ongoing-in-defiance-of-the-law-n2661156,

89. *This statement led*: Alec Schemmel, "Christian university rebranding DEI to evade Trump order, enroll illegals, Tennessee rep says," Fox News, July 18, 2025, https://www.foxnews.com/politics/christian-university-rebranding-dei-evade-trump-order-enroll-illegals-tn-rep-says.

90. *One of those lawyers*: Julian Mark, "He never saw himself as disadvantaged. Then the government had him write an essay," *Washington Post*, June 29, 2024, https://www.washingtonpost.com/business/2024/06/29/sba-8a-curtis-joachim-racial-inequality/.

90. *Legal scholar Justin Driver*: Justin Driver, "The Excruciating Question Confronting Black College Applicants," *New York Times*, September 1, 2025, https://www.nytimes.com/2025/09/01/opinion/college-essay-post-affirmative-action.html.

91. *Yet well-meaning allies*: E.N. Sherf, S. Tangirala, and K.C. Weber, "It is

not my place! Psychological standing and men's voice and participation in gender-parity initiatives," *Organization Science* 28, no. 2 (2017): 193–210, https://doi.org/10.1287/orsc.2017.1118.
92. *One study found that*: David Hekman et al., "Does diversity-valuing behavior result in diminished performance ratings for non-white and female leaders?," *Academy of Management Journal* 60, no. 2 (2017): 771–97, https://doi.org/10.5465/amj.2014.0538.
92. *Other studies have found that*: See, e.g., Jill E. Gulker, Aimee Y. Mark, and Margo J. Monteith, "Confronting prejudice: The *who, what*, and *why* of confrontation effectiveness," *Social Influence* 8, no. 4 (2012): 280–93, https://doi.org/10.1080/15534510.2012.736879; Heather M. Rasinski and Alexander M. Czopp, "The Effect of Target Status on Witnesses' Reactions to Confrontations of Bias," *Basic and Applied Social Psychology* 32, no. 2 (2010): 8–16, https://doi.org/10.1080/01973530903539754.
93. *A newer and now essential*: For more on a conceptual shift from a "zero-sum" frame to a universal frame, see Heather McGhee, *The Sum of Us: What Racism Costs Everyone and How We Can Prosper Together* (New York: One World, 2021).
93. *As the Supreme Court noted*: Students for Fair Admissions, 218–19.
93. *We're troubled whenever*: Taylor Ballinger, Tao Jiang, and Jennifer Crocker, "Lay theories of diversity initiatives: Theory and measurement of zero-sum and win-win beliefs," *Group Processes & Intergroup Relations* 27, no. 4 (September 2023), https://doi.org/10.1177/13684302231193320.
93. *Policy advocate Angela Glover*: Angela Glover Blackwell, "The Curb-Cut Effect," *Stanford Social Innovation Review*, Winter 2017, https://ssir.org/articles/entry/the_curb_cut_effect.
93. *Parental leave*: Alina Dizik, "More dads are taking parental leave than ever. Moms aren't always happy about it," *The Guardian*, February 16, 2024, https://www.theguardian.com/lifeandstyle/2024/feb/16/paternity-maternity-leave-unequal.
93. *In fact, one study*: Troy Dreier, "80% of Video Caption Users Aren't

Hearing Impaired, Finds Verizon," *Streaming Media*, May 20, 2019, https://www.streamingmedia.com/Articles/ReadArticle.aspx?ArticleID=131860.

94. *Many common equality initiatives*: Amy C. Edmondson, *The Fearless Organization: Creating Psychological Safety in the Workplace for Learning, Innovation, and Growth* (Hoboken: John Wiley & Sons, 2019).

94. *On the right*: Jennifer Gratz, "Discriminating Toward Equality: Affirmative Action and the Diversity Charade," The Heritage Foundation, February 27, 2014, https://www.heritage.org/poverty-and-inequality/report/discriminating-toward-equality-affirmative-action-and-the-diversity.

95. *On the left*: Susan Neiman, *Left Is Not Woke* (Cambridge, UK: Polity Press, 2023), 11–56.

95. *And in the center*: Yascha Mounk, *The Identity Trap: A Story of Ideas and Power in Our Time* (New York: Penguin Press, 2023), 183.

95. *Mounk argues that*: Ibid., 199.

95. *In one study*: Markus Brauer and Abdelatif Er-rafiy, "Increasing perceived variability reduces prejudice and discrimination," *Journal of Experimental Social Psychology* 47, no. 5 (September 2011): 871–81, https://doi.org/10.1016/j.jesp.2011.03.003.

STRATEGY 6: RECLAIM MERIT

98. *Michigan Republicans*: "Michigan House passes anti-DEI proposal co-sponsored by Rep. Pavlov," Michigan House Republicans, May 8, 2025, https://gophouse.org/posts/michigan-house-passes-anti-dei-proposal-co-sponsored-by-rep-pavlov.

98. *Democratic Representative*: Rachel Mintz, "Michigan House passes merit-based hiring bill amid debate over DEI hiring," Michigan Public, May 6, 2025, https://www.michiganpublic.org/politics-government/2025-05-06/michigan-house-passes-merit-based-hiring-bill-amid-debate-over-dei-hiring.

98. *Speaking after the vote*: Jessica Guynn, "'Root out DEI': Why red

states are enlisting in Trump's war on 'woke,'" *USA Today*, May 15, 2025, https://www.usatoday.com/story/news/politics/2025/05/15/red-states-join-trump-dei-fight/83518866007/.

98. *As inclusion consultant*: Emma McKee, "DEI is the True Merit-Based System," LinkedIn, January 29, 2025, https://www.linkedin.com/pulse/dei-true-merit-based-system-emma-mckee-khfoe/.

98. *Executive orders*: Exec. Order No. 14281, 90 Fed. Reg. 17537 (April 28, 2025); Exec. Order No. 14173, 90 Fed. Reg. 8633 (January 31, 2025).

99. *Prominent anti-DEI writer*: Heather Mac Donald, "Merit Over Identity," *City Journal*, April 11, 2023, https://www.city-journal.org/article/higher-ed-must-choose-merit-over-identity.

99. *Alison Collins*: Sophie Bearman (@stbearman), "At the heart of these debates is the question of what constitutes fair admissions criteria. On Oct. 13, 2020, Commissioner Alison Collins said that merit is racist and the "antithesis of fair." (3/7)," X, February 2, 2021, https://x.com/stbearman/status/1356649178026233857.

99. *Research has shown*: Marianne Cooper, "The False Promise of Meritocracy," *The Atlantic*, December 1, 2015, https://www.theatlantic.com/business/archive/2015/12/meritocracy/418074/.

99. *His post introduced the concept*: Alexandr Wang (@alexandr_wang), "Today we've formalized an important hiring policy at Scale. We hire for MEI: merit, excellence, and intelligence....," X, June 13, 2024, https://x.com/alexandr_wang/status/1801331034916851995?lang=en.

99. *Other corporate leaders*: Paige McGlauflin, "Elon Musk and other DEI critics are latching on to 'MEI,' a new hiring catchphrase that experts say misses the point," *Fortune*, June 24, 2024, https://fortune.com/2024/06/24/mei-elon-musk-alexandr-wang-anti-dei-hiring-merit-excellence-intelligence/.

99. *By March 2025*: Roland Fryer, "The Economics of DEI and Merit," *Wall Street Journal*, March 6, 2025, https://www.wsj.com/opinion/the-economics-of-dei-and-merit-hiring-productivity-1fc094d2.

100. *The Scale AI CEO*: Alexandr Wang (@alexandr_wang), X, June 13,

100. 2024, https://x.com/alexandr_wang/status/1801331034916851995?lang=en.
100. *In defining MEI*: Ibid.
100. *The Trump administration*: Brian Stelter, "How Pete Hegseth went from Fox News host to Trump's Defense Secretary pick," CNN, November 13, 2024, https://www.cnn.com/2024/11/13/media/pete-hegseth-fox-news-trump-defense-secretary; Max Matza and Mike Wendling, "Trump picks former WWE CEO and TV's Dr Oz for top roles," BBC, November 20, 2024, https://www.bbc.com/news/articles/c8rl8knmg8eo; Clare Malone, "The Junk Science of Robert F. Kennedy, Jr.," *The New Yorker*, January 29, 2025, https://www.newyorker.com/news/the-lede/the-junk-science-of-robert-f-kennedy-jr.
100. *When the legal nonprofit*: "Federal Civil Rights Complaint Challenges Harvard's Legacy Admissions," Lawyers for Civil Rights, accessed August 28, 2025, https://lawyersforcivilrights.org/our-impact/education/federal-civil-rights-complaint-challenges-harvards-legacy-admissions/.
101. *In an illuminating study*: Frank L. Samson, "Multiple Group Threat and Malleable White Attitudes Toward Academic Merit," *Du Bois Review* 10, no. 1 (2013): 233–60, https://doi.org/10.1017/S1742058X1300012X.
102. *As the researcher observed*: Ibid., 253.
102. *In the early twentieth century*: Valerie Strauss, "A brief history of antisemitism in U.S. higher education," *Washington Post*, November 13, 2023, https://www.washingtonpost.com/education/2023/11/13/how-restricting-jews-created-modern-college-admissions/.
102. *The researchers hypothesized*: Emilio J. Castilla and Stephen Benard, "The Paradox of Meritocracy in Organizations," *Administrative Science Quarterly* 55, no. 4 (December 2010): 543–76, https://doi.org/10.2189/asqu.2010.55.4.543.
103. *When participants learned*: Daniela Goya-Tocchetto, Aaron C. Kay, and B. Keith Payne, "Can Selecting the Most Qualified Candidate Be Unfair? Learning About Socioeconomic Advantages and Disadvantages

Reduces the Perceived Fairness of Meritocracy and Increases Support for Socioeconomic Diversity Initiatives in Organizations," *Journal of Experimental Psychology: General* 153, no. 12 (2024): 2962–76, https://doi.org/10.1037/xge0001525.

103. *In his book* Disability Pride: Ben Mattlin, *Disability Pride: Dispatches from a Post-ADA World* (Boston: Beacon Press, 2022).

103. *The sonnet voices*: John Milton, "Sonnet 19: When I Consider How My Light Is Spent," The Poetry Foundation, https://www.poetryfoundation.org/poems/44750/sonnet-19-when-i-consider-how-my-light-is-spent.

103. *Mattlin took inspiration*: Mattlin, *Disability Pride*, 203.

104. *In his book The Tyranny*: Michael J. Sandel, *The Tyranny of Merit: Can We Find the Common Good?* (New York: Farrar, Straus and Giroux, 2020), 180.

104. *Such pressure means*: Ibid., 178.

104. *This result fuels*: Ibid., 24–25.

105. *A novel by Lionel Shriver*: Lionel Shriver, *Mania: A Novel* (New York: HarperCollins, 2024).

106. *They could move away*: Lani Guinier, *The Tyranny of the Meritocracy: Democratizing Higher Education in America* (Boston: Beacon Press, 2015).

106. *Black patients have*: Erika Stallings, "Black patients, black physicians and the need to improve health outcomes for African Americans," NBC News, May 6, 2019, https://www.nbcnews.com/news/nbcblk/black-patients-black-physicians-need-improve-health-outcomes-african-americans-n1000696.

106. *Many argue boys*: Elizabeth Heubeck, "Why Boys Don't Want to Become Teachers and What Schools Can Do About It," *Education Week*, January 27, 2025, https://www.edweek.org/leadership/why-boys-dont-want-to-become-teachers-and-what-schools-can-do-about-it/2025/01.

106. *The accuracy of clinical*: Alice McCarthy, "Embracing Diversity: The Imperative for Inclusive Clinical Trials," Harvard Medical School,

June 30, 2023, https://learn.hms.harvard.edu/insights/all-insights/embracing-diversity-imperative-inclusive-clinical-trials.

106. *Teams composed of people*: Katherine W. Phillips, "How Diversity Makes Us Smarter," *Scientific American*, October 1, 2014, https://www.scientificamerican.com/article/how-diversity-makes-us-smarter/.

106. *These are just a few examples*: In some instances, directly considering diversity factors like race or sex may violate anti-discrimination laws. A lot depends on the type of decision, the entity making the decision, how the diversity factor is considered, and what justification the decision-maker has for considering that factor.

107. *A report by education scholars*: Arthur L. Coleman and Jamie Lewis Keith, "Understanding Holistic Review in Higher Education Admissions: Guiding Principles and Model Illustrations," November 2018, https://highered.collegeboard.org/media/pdf/understanding-holistic-review-he-admissions.pdf, 8.

108. *Even Sandel states*: Sandel, *The Tyranny of Merit*, 33.

108. *To expand economic opportunity*: "Customized Employment," U.S. Department of Labor, accessed August 20, 2025, https://www.dol.gov/agencies/odep/program-areas/cie/customized-employment.

109. *Bob Sternfels*: Ambereen Choudhury and Amy Bainbridge, "McKinsey Champions Diversity While Rivals Abandon Targets," *Bloomberg*, February 12, 2025, https://www.bloomberg.com/news/articles/2025-02-12/mckinsey-strikes-defiant-tone-on-diversity-while-rivals-balk.

109. *The diversity page on its website*: "Merit-Based Diversity, Equity, and Inclusion: Who We Are," Pfizer, accessed August 20, 2025, https://www.pfizer.com/about/responsibility/diversity-and-inclusion.

109. *In one study*: Seval Gündemir et al., "Multicultural meritocracy: The synergistic benefits of valuing diversity *and* merit," *Journal of Experimental Social Psychology* 73 (November 2017): 34–41, https://doi.org/10.1016/j.jesp.2017.06.002.

111. *Some opponents*: John Tierney, "Didn't Earn It," *City Journal*, June 4, 2024, https://www.city-journal.org/article/didnt-earn-it.

111. *Proponents clap back*: D'Angela Proctor, "I Was a Diversity Hire and Here's My Experience," LinkedIn, March 20, 2025, https://www.linkedin.com/pulse/i-diversity-hire-heres-my-experience-d-angela-proctor-esquire-xpjqc/; Matt Brown, "Baltimore mayor fights back against attacks on DEI initiatives with 'Definitely Earned It' campaign," *Associated Press*, February 4, 2025, https://apnews.com/article/dei-baltimore-mayor-trump-definitely-earned-it-f4c8d52981a64dd2125b2e1ee2df631e.

STRATEGY 7: HIGHLIGHT THE RISKS OF RETREAT

114. *One survey of 750*: "1 in 3 Companies That Rolled Back DEI Initiatives Are Reinstating Them," Resume Templates, May 13, 2025, https://www.resumetemplates.com/1-in-3-companies-that-rolled-back-dei-initiatives-are-reinstating-them/.
114. *Each news cycle*: See, e.g., Brian Cheung, "Google rolls back DEI efforts, including hiring goals," NBC News, February 5, 2025, https://www.nbcnews.com/tech/tech-news/google-rolls-back-dei-efforts-hiring-goals-rcna190902; Thomas Barrabi and Ariel Zilber, "Meta, Amazon ditch DEI programs as tech giants move away from 'woke' agenda," *New York Post*, January 10, 2025, https://nypost.com/2025/01/10/business/meta-axes-dei-programs-after-mark-zuckerberg-scrapped-censorship-policies/; Bruce Crumley, "Walmart Joins Growing List of Companies Dropping DEI Policies," *Inc.*, November 26, 2024, https://www.inc.com/bruce-crumley/walmart-joins-growing-list-of-companies-dropping-dei-policies/91024542.
116. *It's true that there's been*: Advancing DEI Initiative (website), accessed August 28, 2025, https://advancingdei.meltzercenter.org/.
116. *In 2025, our center*: Alixandra Pollack, David Glasgow, Tara Van Bommel PhD, Christina Joseph, and Kenji Yoshino, *Risks of retreat: The enduring inclusion imperative*, Catalyst and Meltzer Center for Diversity, Inclusion, and Belonging, June 11, 2025, https://www.catalyst.org/insights/2025/risks-of-retreat-report.

116. *In 2025, Verizon*: Maria Aspan, "Verizon ends DEI policies to get FCC's blessing for its $20 billion Frontier deal," NPR, May 19, 2025, https://www.npr.org/2025/05/19/nx-s1-5402863/verizon-fcc-frontier-dei-trump.

117. *He noted that the Commission*: Cameron Marx, "CPUC Raises Concerns Over Verizon's Rollback of DEI Programs," *Broadband Breakfast*, July 28, 2025, https://broadbandbreakfast.com/cpuc-raises-concerns-over-verizons-rollback-of-dei-programs/.

117. *In the spring of 2023*: Dylan Mulvaney (@dylanmulvaney), "Happy March Madness!! Just found out this had to do with sports and not just saying it's a crazy month! In celebration of this sports thing @budlight is giving you the chance to win $15,000! Share a video with #EasyCarryContest for a chance to win!! Good luck! #budlightpartner," Instagram, April 1, 2023, https://www.instagram.com/reel/CqgTftujqZc/?utm_source=ig_embed&ig_rid=287d342a-e120-42c6-927f-d764b1befaff.

117. *Prominent conservatives blasted*: Lindsay Dodgson, "Conservatives called for a boycott of Bud Light after it partnered with trans influencer Dylan Mulvaney. The company stood by its choice," *Yahoo News*, April 6, 2023, https://www.yahoo.com/news/conservatives-called-boycott-bud-light-102020126.html.

117. *In a totally normal*: Kid Rock (@kidrock), Instagram, April 3, 2023, https://www.instagram.com/p/CqmUBDegYwN/?img_index=1.

117. *Two of the company's*: Jennifer Maloney, "Bud Light Maker Offers Distributors Free Beer, More Ad Spending After Dylan Mulvaney Backlash," *Wall Street Journal*, May 2, 2023, https://www.wsj.com/us-news/society/bud-light-maker-offers-distributors-free-beer-more-ad-spending-after-dylan-mulvaney-backlash-14efac22?mod=hp_lista_pos1.

117. *Bud Light's market*: Grace Mayer, "Bud Light backlash: How the fallout from the Dylan Mulvaney promotion started, and all the chaos that ensued," *Business Insider*, August 18, 2023, https://www.businessinsider.com/bud-light-transgender-controversy-backlash-boycotts-history.

NOTES

117. *"Go woke, go broke"*: Hugh Cameron, "Disney Layoffs Celebrated by Critics: 'Go Woke Go Broke,'" *Newsweek*, June 3, 2025, https://www.newsweek.com/disney-layoffs-celebrated-go-woke-go-broke-2080183.

118. *Starbuck, who has*: Nathaniel Meyersohn, "The right-wing activist riding a wave of opposition to DEI in corporate America," CNN, August 28, 2024, https://www.cnn.com/2024/08/28/business/dei-john-deere-harley-davidson-robby-starbuck/index.html.

118. *"No more DEI departments"*: Jessica Guynn, "Inside Robby Starbuck's anti-DEI war on Tractor Supply, John Deere and Harley-Davidson," *USA Today*, August 27, 2024, https://www.usatoday.com/story/money/2024/08/02/robby-starbuck-harley-davidson-john-deere-dei/74608637007/.

118. *In January 2025*: "Target's Belonging at the Bullseye Strategy," Target, January 24, 2025, https://corporate.target.com/press/fact-sheet/2025/01/belonging-bullseye-strategy.

118. *This statement sparked*: Stacy M. Brown, "Black Press, Shoppers Turn Up Heat on Target," *The Atlanta Voice*, June 22, 2025, https://theatlantavoice.com/target-dei-backlash-boycott-slow-sales/.

118. *An Atlanta megachurch pastor*: Monica Torres, "Black and Latine Shoppers Continue to Boycott Target—And It Might Be Working. Here's Why," *Huffpost*, April 28, 2025, https://www.huffpost.com/entry/target-boycott_l_680a884ae4b042d124856ce9.

118. *"We will break"*: Jeff Green, "Pastor Sees Boycott of Target Stores as New Civil Rights Fight," *Bloomberg*, August 12, 2025, https://www.bloomberg.com/news/features/2025-08-12/atlanta-pastor-sees-target-store-boycott-as-new-civil-rights-fight.

118. *Foot traffic to Target's stores*: Andrew Adam Newman, "Target foot-traffic falls for fifth straight month since backtracking on DEI," *Retail Brew*, July 16, 2025, https://www.retailbrew.com/stories/2025/07/16/target-foot-traffic-falls-for-fifth-straight-month-since-backtracking-on-dei.

118. *Its share price*: Sarah Bregel, "Target stock tumbles again as customer

backlash over its DEI rollback takes a bite out of sales," *Fast Company*, May 21, 2025, https://www.fastcompany.com/91338591/target-stock-price-backlash-to-dei-rollback-hits-sales-shares-down.

118. *One consumer research firm*: Terry Tang, "Pro-DEI organizers fired up to maintain Target boycott as promises go unfulfilled," Associated Press, August 27, 2025, https://apnews.com/article/target-walmart-ceo-boycott-dei-7996ce3fbf7f0cc9207472bc7a227cd6.

119. *On an earnings call*: Brooke DiPalma and Alexis Keenan, "DEI boycott 'played a role' in Target's Q1 sales slump as foot traffic declined," Yahoo Finance, May 21, 2025, https://finance.yahoo.com/news/dei-boycott-played-a-role-in-targets-q1-sales-slump-as-foot-traffic-declined-183135827.html.

119. *Advocates have also urged*: Doc Louallen, "National boycott targets McDonald's after rolling back diversity initiatives," ABC News, June 24, 2025, https://abcnews.go.com/Business/national-boycott-targets-mcdonalds-after-rolling-back-diversity/story?id=123161784; "The People's Union USA" (website), accessed August 20, 2025, https://thepeoplesunionusa.com/boycott-list; Betty Lin-Fisher, "Black church leader calls for electronic protest of Dollar General over DEI retreat," *USA Today*, May 28, 2025, https://www.usatoday.com/story/money/2025/05/28/dollar-general-boycott-electronic-protest-dei/83678827007/.

119. Axios *concluded*: Eleanor Hawkins, "Companies that kept DEI commitments saw higher reputation scores in 2025," *Axios*, May 29, 2025, https://www.axios.com/2025/05/29/dei-patagonia-costco-microsoft-reputation-surge.

119. *In our research with Catalyst*: Pollack et al., *Risks of retreat.*

120. *Indeed, a July 2025*: "6 in 10 Companies That Eliminated DEI Since Trump's Reelection Are Hiring Fewer Diverse Employees," Resume.org, July 23, 2025, https://www.resume.org/6-in-10-companies-that-eliminated-dei-since-trumps-reelection-are-hiring-fewer-diverse-employees/.

120. *In March 2025*: James Frater and Olesya Dmitracova, "US embassies to contractors worldwide: Cancel any diversity programs or risk going

unpaid," CNN, April 1, 2025, https://www.cnn.com/2025/04/01/business/us-embassies-european-suppliers-dei-intl.

120. 000 *France's gender equality minister*: Kate Plummer, "France Reacts to Donald Trump's DEI Ultimatum," *Newsweek*, March 31, 2025, https://www.newsweek.com/donald-trump-dei-france-2052936.

120. *Belgium's foreign minister*: "Certain foreign firms must 'self-certify' with Trump diversity rules: US embassies," *France 24*, April 2, 2025, https://www.france24.com/en/live-news/20250402-certain-foreign-firms-must-self-certify-with-trump-diversity-rules-us-embassies.

120. *The Spanish Labor Ministry*: "US embassies tell suppliers to comply with Trump ban on diversity policies," Reuters, March 31, 2025, https://www.reuters.com/world/us-embassies-globally-tell-suppliers-comply-with-trump-ban-diversity-policies-2025-03-31/.

120. *On the other side*: Louis Goss, "Khan blocks US consultancy from TFL contracts over diversity clash," *The Telegraph*, April 10, 2025, https://www.telegraph.co.uk/business/2025/04/10/sadiq-khan-blocks-us-consultant-tfl-contracts-diversity/.

121. *Accenture had announced*: "Accenture scraps diversity and inclusion goals, memo says," *The Guardian*, February 8, 2025, https://www.theguardian.com/accenture/2025/feb/08/accenture-scraps-diversity-and-inclusion-goals-memo-says.

121. *It stated through a spokesperson*: Louis Goss, "Khan blocks US consultancy from TFL contracts over diversity clash," *The Telegraph*, April 10, 2025, https://www.telegraph.co.uk/business/2025/04/10/sadiq-khan-blocks-us-consultant-tfl-contracts-diversity/.

121. *The legislation requires*: Kristy Edser et al., "Australia enacts world 1st workplace gender equality targets mandate," MinterEllison, April 2, 2025, https://www.minterellison.com/articles/australia-enacts-workplace-gender-equality-targets; "Targets: Frequently Asked Questions," Workplace Gender Equality Agency, July 31, 2025, https://www.wgea.gov.au/about/our-legislation/targets.

121. *But the U.S. order*: Kristy Edser et al., "Australia enacts world 1st workplace gender equality targets mandate," MinterEllison, April 2,

2025, https://www.minterellison.com/articles/australia-enacts-workplace-gender-equality-targets.

121. *Brazil passed an Equal Pay Act*: Aline Fidelis et al., "Focus on: Brazilian DEI Landscape: Changes to the Brazilian Labor Regulation on Diversity and Inclusion Matters," Legal500, https://www.legal500.com/doing-business-in/brazilian-dei-landscape-changes-to-the-brazilian-labor-regulation-on-diversity-and-inclusion-matters/.

121. *It also pushed*: Marcela Ayres and Bernardo Caram, "Brazil to push social diversity as criteria for sustainable investments at COP30," Reuters, February 6, 2025, https://www.reuters.com/world/americas/brazil-push-social-diversity-criteria-sustainable-investments-cop30-2025-02-06/.

121. *As one observed*: Kiyoshi Takenaka, "Most Japan firms stay committed to diversity despite US moves, Reuters survey shows," Reuters, March 20, 2025, https://www.reuters.com/world/japan/most-japan-firms-stay-committed-diversity-despite-us-moves-reuters-survey-shows-2025-03-20/.

122. *At the very least*: Benn Dummett and Joe Wallace, "'Anti-Woke' in the U.S., DEI at Home: the New Playbook for European Companies," *Wall Street Journal*, March 20, 2025, https://www.wsj.com/business/anti-woke-in-the-u-s-dei-at-home-the-new-playbook-for-european-companies-0461e6a9.

123. *A 2023 Pew survey*: Rachel Minkin, "Diversity, Equity, and Inclusion in the Workplace," Pew Research Center, May 17, 2023, https://www.pewresearch.org/social-trends/2023/05/17/diversity-equity-and-inclusion-in-the-workplace/.

123. *A 2024 Gallup poll*: "Bentley-Gallup Business in Society Survey 2024 Report," accessed August 20, 2025, https://bentleydownloads.s3.amazonaws.com/general/2024+Bentley_Gallup+Business+in+Society+Report.pdf, 10; "Views on DEI, Trans Rights, Higher Education, and AI | National Poll - April 22, 2025," UMassAmherst (accessed August 20, 2025), https://www.umass.edu/political-science/about/reports/2025-8#toc-toplines-and-crosstabs.

123. *As journalist Simone Foxman*: Simone Foxman, "What Went Wrong

for DEI?," *Bloomberg*, March 21, 2025, https://www.bloomberg.com/news/features/2025-03-21/who-killed-dei-before-trump-s-executive-orders-companies-overpromised.
124. *Writing in 2025*: Callum Borchers, "Companies Quietly Recast DEI to Duck Backlash," *Wall Street Journal*, June 11, 2025, https://www.wsj.com/lifestyle/careers/company-dei-strategies-d859e7d7.
124. *Of particular note*: Frank Dobbin, *Inventing Equal Opportunity* (Princeton: Princeton University Press, 2009), 133–60.

CONCLUSION

127. *Derived from words*: Adrienne Matei, "Nostalgia's unexpected etymology explains why it can feel so painful," *Quartz*, July 20, 2022, https://qz.com/1108120/nostalgias-unexpected-etymology-explains-why-it-can-feel-so-painful.
127. *The administration effectively ended*: "No More Refugees, Trump Said. Except White South Africans," *The Daily Podcast*, May 19, 2025, https://www.nytimes.com/2025/05/19/podcasts/the-daily/refugees-trump-white-south-africans-afrikaners.html?showTranscript=1.
127. *It ordered a comprehensive review*: "Letter to the Smithsonian: Internal Review of Smithsonian Exhibitions and Materials," The White House, August 12, 2025, https://www.whitehouse.gov/briefings-statements/2025/08/letter-to-the-smithsonian-internal-review-of-smithsonian-exhibitions-and-materials/; Exec. Order No. 14253, 90 Fed. Reg. 14563 (April 3, 2025).
127. *It ordered the restoration*: Ashraf Khalil, "Confederate statues in DC area to be restored and replaced in line with Trump's executive order," Associated Press, August 5, 2025, https://apnews.com/article/confederate-statue-removal-replacement-trump-culture-13ae94da5a9d-652ba8a678d24bc9e7e8; Joe Walsh and Eleanor Watson, "Trump says he's restoring the original Confederate names of these Army bases—but with new namesakes," CBS News, June 11, 2025, https://www.cbsnews.com/news/trump-restoring-confederate-names-army-bases/;

NOTES

Eleanor Watson et al., "Navy set to rename USNS Harvey Milk, mulls new names for other ships named for civil rights leaders," CBS News, June 3, 2025, https://www.cbsnews.com/news/navy-new-name-usns-harvey-milk-ships-named-for-civil-rights-leaders/.

128. *It appointed Christian nationalists*: Adam Gabbatt, "Trump has put Christian nationalists in key roles—say a prayer for free speech," *The Guardian*, April 16, 2025, https://www.theguardian.com/us-news/2025/apr/16/christian-nationalists-trump-administration.

128. *It sanitized*: Jon Swaine and Jeremy B. Merrill, "Amid anti-DEI push, National Park Service rewrites history of Underground Railroad," *Washington Post*, April 6, 2025, https://www.washingtonpost.com/investigations/2025/04/06/national-park-service-underground-railroad-history-slavery/; Sara Ruberg, "National Park Service Restores Web Page Featuring Harriet Tubman," *New York Times*, April 8, 2025, https://www.nytimes.com/2025/04/08/us/politics/national-park-service-harriet-tubman-underground-railroad-dei.html; Tim Balk, "Jackie Robinson's Legacy Vanishes, Then Reappears, on Pentagon Site," *New York Times*, March 19, 2025, https://www.nytimes.com/2025/03/19/us/politics/jackie-robinson-defense-department.html.

128. *President Trump issued*: Exec. Order No. 14190, 90 Fed. Reg. 8853 (February 3, 2025).

128. *He took over*: Jennifer Jacobs and Kathryn Wilson, "How Trump is reshaping the Kennedy Center, moving away from 'woke culture,'" CBS News, February 13, 2025, https://www.cbsnews.com/news/trump-reshaping-kennedy-center-board-performances/.

128. *Often, this project*: Stephanie Coontz, *The Way We Never Were: American Families and the Nostalgia Trap* (New York: Basic Books, 1992).

128. *In 2015, President Barack Obama*: Julie Hirschfeld Davis, "Mount McKinley Will Again Be Called Denali," *New York Times*, August 30, 2015, https://www.nytimes.com/2015/08/31/us/mount-mckinley-will-be-renamed-denali.html.

128. *Yet President Trump*: Exec. Order No. 14172, 90 Fed. Reg. 8629 (January 31, 2025).

128. *No surprise, then*: Dennis E. Curtis and Judith Resnik, "Images of Justice," *Yale Law Journal* 96 (1986–87), 1742.

129. *It would be a mistake*: For more on left-wing nostalgia, see Agnes Arnold-Forster, *Nostalgia: A History of a Dangerous Emotion* (London: Picador, 2024), 173–88.

129. *As columnist Jamelle Bouie*: Jamelle Bouie, "Trump Is on the Wrong Side of History by Design," *New York Times*, February 12, 2025, https://www.nytimes.com/2025/02/12/opinion/trump-dei-meritocracy-civil-right.html.

129. *Proponents of equality should feel*: Lyndon B. Johnson, "Radio and Television Remarks Upon Signing the Civil Rights Bill," The American Presidency Project, https://www.presidency.ucsb.edu/documents/radio-and-television-remarks-upon-signing-the-civil-rights-bill.

131. *He won a series of cases*: "Timeline of Events Leading to the Brown v. Board of Education Decision of 1954," National Archives, accessed August 28, 2025, https://www.archives.gov/education/lessons/brown-v-board/timeline.html.

131. *Marshall's pragmatic*: Jeffrey Rosen, "Ruth Bader Ginsburg Is an American Hero," *The New Republic*, September 28, 2014, https://newrepublic.com/article/119578/ruth-bader-ginsburg-interview-retirement-feminists-jazzercise; Sheryl Gay Stolberg, "In Fight for Marriage Rights, 'She's Our Thurgood Marshall,'" *New York Times*, March 27, 2013, https://www.nytimes.com/2013/03/28/us/maine-lawyer-credited-in-fight-for-gay-marriage.html.

132. *Yet as Chugh points out*: Dolly Chugh, *The Person You Mean to Be: How Good People Fight Bias* (New York: HarperCollins, 2018), xxiv–xxvi.

132. *But as psychologist*: Jamil Zaki, *Hope for Cynics: The Surprising Science of Human Goodness* (New York: Grand Central Publishing, 2024), 7.

132. *In the 1970s*: Maria Godoy, "Dolores Huerta: The Civil Rights Icon Who Showed Farmworkers 'Si Se Puede,'" NPR, September 17, 2017, https://www.npr.org/sections/thesalt/2017/09/17/551490281/dolores-huerta-the-civil-rights-icon-who-showed-farmworkers-si-se-puede.

READING GROUP GUIDE

These questions are intended for book clubs, educational institutions, and workplaces that wish to host small-group discussions around the content of *How Equality Wins*.

1. The authors describe a dramatic shift in the zeitgeist over a short time span. After the murder of George Floyd in 2020, leaders felt tremendous pressure to advance the values of diversity and equality and to publicly showcase their efforts. Only a few years later, some commentators were declaring DEI "dead." What made opponents of DEI so effective in shifting the culture?

2. The authors offer seven strategies for reforming the work of DEI so the "project of equality" can endure. Which strategies resonated with you the most and least? Why?

3. In Strategy 1: Reveal the Stakes, the authors describe the DEI debate using the metaphor of a room: proponents of the project of equality are standing on one side of the room, opponents are standing on the opposite side, and both groups are trying to convince the people standing in the middle of the room to move over to their side. In your experience, what arguments are most effective in persuading the people in the middle?

4. In Strategy 2: Support Dissent, the authors argue that the pro-equality community needs to embrace free speech, welcome dissent, and fix its tendency to shame people for mistakes. Have

you experienced any of the dogmatic or shaming behavior they criticize in this chapter? If so, what effect did that behavior have on you? If not, why do you think this is such a common complaint against the DEI community?

5. In Strategy 3: Welcome New Groups, the authors discuss a core tension within the project of equality: it's not possible to include every group in society, but it's also not reasonable to be closed to new group claims. What metrics would you use to decide whether a new social group should be recognized by the project of equality? Which new groups do you think need to be included?

6. In Strategy 4: Level the Playing Field, the authors argue that a shift from "lifting" to "leveling" makes the project of equality narrower, but it could also make the project deeper. Think of the organizations you're involved in, whether as an employee, student, volunteer, or otherwise. What "deep" equality work could be done in those organizations?

7. In Strategy 5: Embrace the Universal, the authors discuss how opening up "targeted programs" to allow anyone to participate could help mitigate a "zero-sum" mindset that causes people to oppose equality programs. Do you agree? If so, why? If not, how would you tackle the zero-sum thinking that drives opposition to DEI?

8. In Strategy 6: Reclaim Merit, the authors accept some critiques of the concept of "merit," but nonetheless conclude that the project of equality must embrace merit for both strategic and principled reasons. What was your reaction to the "more nuanced and humane vision" of merit that the authors sketch?

9. In Strategy 7: Highlight the Risks of Retreat, the authors argue that all the focus on the risks of DEI has caused people to underestimate the risks of retreating from the project of equality. Of

the four risks they discuss (legal risks, reputational risks, global risks, and temporal risks), which (if any) was most convincing to you as a reason to stick with the project of equality, and why?

10. Were any important strategies missing from the book? If you could reform the project of equality, what changes would you make?

11. How, if at all, will the strategies recommended in this book change how you approach your own efforts to advance organizational equality?

12. As you consider the future of equality, do you feel cynical, hopeful, or some combination of the two? Why?

ABOUT THE AUTHORS

Kenji Yoshino is the Chief Justice Earl Warren Professor of Constitutional Law at NYU School of Law and the director of the Meltzer Center for Diversity, Inclusion, and Belonging. A graduate of Harvard, Oxford, and Yale Law School, he specializes in constitutional law and antidiscrimination law. He received tenure at Yale Law School, where he served as deputy dean before moving to NYU. Yoshino has published in major academic journals, including the *Harvard Law Review* and the *Yale Law Journal*. He has also written for more popular forums, including the *New York Times* and the *Washington Post*. Yoshino is the author or coauthor of four previous books—most recently, *Say the Right Thing: How to Talk About Identity, Diversity, and Justice* (coauthored with David Glasgow) was published by Simon & Schuster in February 2023. Yoshino has served as the president of the Harvard Board of Overseers. He currently serves on the board of the Brennan Center for Justice, the NAACP Legal Defense Fund, and Meta's Oversight Board. He also serves on advisory boards for diversity and inclusion for Morgan Stanley and Charter Communications. He has won numerous awards for his teaching and scholarship, including the American Bar Association's Silver Gavel Award, the Peck Medal in Jurisprudence, and New York University's Distinguished Teaching Award. He and his family live in Manhattan.

David Glasgow is the founding executive director of the Meltzer Center for Diversity, Inclusion, and Belonging, an adjunct professor at New York University School of Law, and coauthor (with Kenji Yoshino) of the book *Say the Right Thing: How to Talk about Identity, Diversity, and Justice*. A nationally recognized expert on allyship as well as the law of diversity, equity, and inclusion, David has written for a range of publications including the *American Journal of Law and Equality*, the *Los Angeles Times*, the *Boston Globe*, *TIME*, and the *Harvard Business Review*. He was the lead author on Black Theatre United's "A New Deal for Broadway," a historic agreement to transform the commercial theater industry. An attorney in New York and Australia, David has a BA in Philosophy and an LLB from the University of Melbourne, Australia, and a Master of Laws (LLM) from NYU School of Law. Prior to his role at the Meltzer Center, he practiced employment, labor relations, and antidiscrimination law at international law firm King & Wood Mallesons, and clerked on the Federal Court of Australia.